Anonymus

Insurance in California

Anonymus

Insurance in California

ISBN/EAN: 9783743344709

Manufactured in Europe, USA, Canada, Australia, Japa

Cover: Foto ©ninafisch / pixelio.de

Manufactured and distributed by brebook publishing software
(www.brebook.com)

Anonymus

Insurance in California

INSURANCE * * *

* * * IN CALIFORNIA.

1849–1888.

SAN FRANCISCO.
Commercial Publishing Company, Publishers.
1888.

Preface.

A Complete history of Insurance in California from its inception would fill a bulky volume, and like every thing connected with the Pioneer period of this State, particularly in its marine branch, would be of the deepest interest to the outside public, as well as to the profession. In the limited scope of this work it has been impossible to give more than an outline of the early insurance methods and sketches of some of the Pioneers, together with a few anecdotes bearing on the subject. For the generous encouragement rendered us by the profession we hereby tender grateful acknowledgement and particularly desire to thank Messrs. Casper T. Hopkins, J. S. Bacon, M. M. Rohrer, and Col. C. L. Taylor for the valuable assistance rendered us in obtaining the data contained in the following pages.

THE PUBLISHERS.

Pioneer Days.

CHAPTER I.

EVEN a brief sketch of the earlier insurance business of San Francisco, causes the writer to delve in such a labyrinth of statistics, such ponderous files of old newspapers and periodicals, replete with interesting facts not connected with insurance, that one requires the utmost care not to fly the track. Here an editorial breathing passionate hatred to the Abolitionist comes into view, or there some astute editor, full of knowledge and statistics, conclusively proves an overland railroad an impossibility. Even the advertising columns of the papers offer allurements that make it next to impossible to follow the track of insurance progress, as they tempt one into the by-ways of speculation as to what has become of that merchant so prominently noticed, or to mark the first modest announcement of some young merchant, now for years at the front of his competitors, laden with wealth and honors. Here again some deed of the Hounds, there the loss of some vessel freighted with hopeful Pioneers or some financial panic or political excitement, leads him from the straight path of duty. It is amid such temptations to wander, that the following data have been collated, and but for the generous assistance of some of the Pioneers in the business, to whom credit is individually given in the preface for their generous and able assistance, it is quite probable this book, if completed at all, would have been deficient in much that through the kindness of those friends it now contains.

The idea of forming local companies in San Francisco was first broached in the fall of 1849 by Barling & McKee, a firm consisting of two enterprising young men from Baltimore. But the suggestion was premature. The State Constitution had not yet been adopted, nor, of course, any legislation enacted providing for the formation of corporations. But in those days the elements of growth were full of life. Before the close of that eventful year, the Constitution was framed and adopted and at the meeting of the first Legislature held under it, an insurance statute entitled "An Act to provide for the formation of Mutual Insurance Companies" was passed. Another law on the same subject was enacted in the spring of 1851. It is a singular fact that legislation on Insurance in California preceded the first statute providing for the incorporation of any kind of Banking Association by more than ten years. It was not until 1859, or about the time when the first timid attempts were made to form Insurance Companies under the statutes of 1850 and 1851, that the first Savings Bank law was passed.

The causes for the delay in establishing in corporate form both of these great interests were to be found in the Constitution itself, whose framers had a holy horror of the wild cat corporations which had played havoc with banking and insurance in the Mississippi Valley. So they provided generally that stockholders in corporations should be individually and personally liable for all the debts of the corporation, without stating whether that liability should be joint or several; and they denied to the Legislature the power to pass any law which should confer upon corporations "any of the privileges of banking," without defining what they meant by "the privileges of banking." The result was that for more than ten years all the banking in the State was done by private firms or the agencies of non-resident bankers, to the great damage of the public through frauds and failures; while the Insurance business was entirely relegated to foreign companies, though with a less disastrous outcome.

Wholesale conflagrations in San Francisco, Sacramento, and in fact in all the pioneer settlements, marked the first four years of the history of the State, inclusive of 1849. The only building material in the seaboard cities was Eastern pine, imported via Cape Horn. Cotton lining, stove pipe chimneys, and camphine lamps created everywhere frightful internal hazards, which were multiplied by the close juxtaposition of hundreds of temporary and inflammable structures in every block and town. So when one burned they all burned. Water was scarce—being supplied only by cisterns at the street corners, which were filled by means of carts. Volunteer fire departments there indeed were, composed of active and courageous young men, but these were supplied only with hand engines, and the men assembled and got to work only by the ringing of alarm bells and after the fire had got well started. There was no profitable field offered for fire insurance under these circumstances.

In marine insurance the conditions were fully as hazardous, for the port was filled with old rotten vessels that came hither on their last voyage. There was no cargo for outward bound ships. The coast was unsurveyed and unmapped from San Diego to Alaska and incorrectly charted south of the Mexican line. In fact, private efforts at exploration and navigation lined the whole West coast with wrecks. The losses of Eastern underwriters in these ventures were enormous, and so frequent were the damages to inward cargoes, owing to the long voyages and the age and unfitness of the vessels employed, that claims were made by almost every ship, and the offices of Port Warden, Underwriters Agent, and Adjuster were worked for all there was in them.

In 1852, after six serious conflagrations in San Francisco had swept away the tents, pine board shanties, hulks of dismantled ships and other similar structures that gave variety and a certain picturesqueness, if not beauty, to San Francisco, brick buildings began to make their appearance. The style of those buildings was fireproof. Thick walls, heavy parapets, brick, earth and metal roofs, substantial iron coverings to every opening, often doubled, and sometimes tiled floors, were the protection against fires availed of by every store and warehouse. When a sufficient number of these had been erected to afford a fair basis for a fire insurance business, the Liverpool and London Fire and Life Insurance Co. appeared in San Francisco, with General Joshua P. Haven as its agent, and in 1853 commenced a cautious business on and in these fireproof buildings.

At that time the assets of the Liverpool and London, all told, were about $3,000,000. Its agent, "Josh Haven," as he was popularly called, was a prominent character in pioneer days, and as he was the first fire and marine underwriter and marine adjuster in San Francisco, both in point of time and in the position he maintained for ten years, it is fitting that his memory should be preserved in these pages.

Joshua P. Haven was a native of Philadelphia, where he was educated in the insurance business. He arrived in San Francisco early in June, 1849, by steamer via Panama, being then 40 years old. He was rather a small man in height and weight, dark complexioned, with large restless black eyes, a large and mobile mouth, a deep, strong voice, and a highly nervous organization. He was extremely social and convivial, full of wit and rollicking fun, thoroughly loyal to his friends, but guiltless of malice towards his enemies, of whom he had his share, being a man of positive views. He was energetic, "by jerks" as sailors say, a regular driver when work had to be done, and possessed of that personal magnetism that characterizes a natural leader of men. He was therefore prominent in public matters; was good at an off-hand speech, especially after dinner; was once a member of the City Council; was a General and one of the early organizers of the State militia. He was liberal and generous to a fault, a connoisseur in good living, a free and easy boon companion with congenial souls. Quick and impulsive by nature and possessed of the intuitive faculty in a marked degree he would see at a glance through the knottiest problems in marine adjustments. He therefore was the Mentor of the shipping interest, and enjoyed for a while almost a monopoly of the adjustment business.

His most memorable case was that of the ship "John Land" which put into Tahiti on fire, damaged much cargo in extinguishing the flames, and transhipped the balance in other vessels, which claimed salvage &c. &c. He settled this case to the satisfaction of all parties, and received a fee of $5,000 for his services.

Haven was not long in building up a premium income of $10,000 per month for the Liverpool and London, nearly all of which was clear profit. His first heavy loss was for $12,000 on the ship-chandlery stock of J. D. Farwell & Co., on Clay Street near Front. This was in 1856. His next serious loss was in the fall of the same year at Marysville. It was a stock of wholesale groceries, insured for $30,000, for Wm. Hawley & Co., in a strictly fire-proof two-story brick building. This had been set on fire at night in a "Norther" by the burning of a barn, 150 feet to windward, the flames from which, driven by the gale like a blow pipe, had found entrance through the melting of the glass in a skylight. The firm was of A 1 standing, the stock worth $75,000, and everything a total loss. Haven's style of handling such a case, maybe inferred from the manner in which the adjustment was made.

Arriving by stage from Sacramento the second morning after the fire, he took a carriage for the ruins. Being there introduced to Mr. Hawley the following talk settled the business.

Haven. "Well Hawley! seems to have been a total loss, eh? What was the value of your stock on the day before the fire?"

Hawley. "About $75,000."

Haven. "Did you save your books?"

Hawley. "No sir, everything burned up clean."

Haven. "Any other insurance?"

Hawley. "No sir."

Haven. "Well, I suppose you would swear to these facts if necessary?"

Hawley. "Certainly sir. Any information I can give you is entirely at your service, but I have no documentary proof to offer."

Haven. "All right sir. This is entirely sufficient. Jump into the carriage sir and come with me to the bank. I will give you a draft for your loss in a moment — I only wish it had occurred in San Francisco."

And in half an hour after his arrival the loss was paid and the business closed up!

Haven had a clerk, a German named Moeller, who wrote a beautiful hand and to whom he left the care of his office business, without security or supervision of any kind. To recoup his losses at play, Moeller frequently failed to enter in the register the policies he issued, quietly pocketing the premiums. At length, a customer applied for a renewal, during Moeller's absence at lunch, of one of those unregistered policies. Haven, unable to find the record of the risk, asked Moeller about it on his return, who excused himself on the ground of omission to enter it, but that night he committed suicide. A subsequent examination showed Haven that many such policies were in existence, but instead of publishing that fact, or informing the company of the defalcation, he took the whole matter on his own shoulders and printed a beautiful obituary notice of his deceased friend.

Pioneer Days.

Mr. Haven was the first resident agent of the Philadelphia Marine Underwriters, and as such had charge of salvage operations in several notable wrecks.

He was a staunch friend of Captain James Alden of the steam revenue cutter Active, formerly the steamer Gold Hunter, plying on the Sacramento river. She was purchased by the United States Government and altered to suit the revenue service. Captain Alden is now Commodore Alden of the U. S. N. It was the custom of Mr. Haven to introduce the cutter as of great service in wrecking expeditions, a gratuitous service, usually rewarded by the underwriters. In case of the clipper ship Carrier Pigeon, on the point of land south of San Francisco that has since borne its name, Mr. Haven was desirous of having the Active go to the scene of the wreck; but the Boston Agent of Underwriters could see no necessity for it, as no danger surrounded the wreck, and there was no use for a cutter's services with its subsequent reward, and respectfully declined to make use of the cutter. This little incident caused for a while some feeling on the part of Mr. Haven, on account of what he termed the parsimony of the Underwriters Agent, who had failed to recognize the usefulness of the revenue cutter.

Mr. Haven also obtained the marine agency of the old Insurance Company of North America, and did a little business for that venerable corporation. But this did not last long. He was very unsystematic in his methods, and one day he wrote $8,000 on the hull of the little high pressure steamboat Sagamore, running between San Francisco and Stockton, omitting to use the "steamboat clause," which would have exonerated the insurers from loss by explosion. The boat blew up at the wharf, killing some eighty persons. Mr. Haven refused to pay the loss, but the company was successfully sued for the sum insured, and then withdrew from the State, remaining out for twenty years after.

In 1855 Mr. Haven associated his half brother, Richard S. Haven, with himself in his agencies, under the firm name of J. P. & R. S. Haven. Richard was an excellent office man and a good adjuster. In many respects he resembled his brother, but not in appearance, he being a decided blonde, nor was he of anything like so positive a temperament. The partnership was dissolved early in 1857. Richard went into business on his own account as agent for the Provincial of Canada, and of the Columbian (Marine) of New York, both of which failed a few years later. He also became popular as an adjuster—at his brother's expense. But he was too amiable to make or keep money either for himself or his principals.

On the dissolution of the firm, J. P. Haven took as his partner William B. Johnston of New York, who ultimately succeeded him as the Resident Secretary of the Liverpool and London, and was for many years a leader in the Insurance world of the Pacific.

Mr. Haven's temperament was just of the kind that makes a man his own worst enemy. The Company had reason to be dissatisfied with his management, and on examination into his affairs, by the New York Secretary in person, he was obliged to turn over the brick building on Montgomery St. (afterward occupied by the Company for many years) in order to balance his accounts, and also to surrender the agency to Mr. Johnston. His adjusting business passed into the hands of R. S. Haven, Gustave Touchard, and Thos. N. Cazneau. Joseph S. Bacon long the agent of the Boston Marine Board of Underwriters succeeded him as agent of the Philadelphia Marine Board of Underwriters. Capt. John T. Hoyt came out from New York to assume the agency of the Marine Underwriters of that port, and Mr. Haven broken down in health and spirits, died in 1862, so poor that all he left to his family was a life policy for $5,000, which had been saved from forfeiture by the kindness of a friend who advanced the last premium.

The Imperial Fire and Life Insurance Company established its fire agency in San Francisco in 1854 in the hands of that sterling old English commission house, Falkner, Bell & Co. who retained it for thirty years, during which the *personnelle* of the San Francisco partners entirely changed. The Monarch Fire and Life Insurance Company of England, long since merged in the Liverpool & London, soon followed; its agent being Wm. Lane Booker, then and for many subsequent years British Consul at San Francisco; thence promoted in 1883 to be Consul General of her Britannic Majesty for the United States, with headquarters in New York. Mr. Booker continued to represent one or more of the best British Fire Companies during his entire residence in San Francisco.

The Northern Fire and Life Insurance Company, of Edinburgh, established its branch on the Pacific Coast in 1854, in the hands of the Scotch commission house of Smith Bros. & Co.

The Home Insurance Company, of New York, commissioned Case, Heiser & Co., of San Francisco, as its agents, and the Continental of the same city appointed C. Adolphe Low & Co. about 1854 or 1855; but neither of these American companies did much business at that early period, their capitals then being only $500,000 each, while all the English companies claiming assets by the million, received the preference from California patrons.

Several short lived mutual fire insurance companies sprang into existence about this time, the first which the advertising columns of the city papers records being the California Mutual, which was confidently floated in August 1853, by Mr. Fontagnene Manager, and Jas. E. C. de Malye Secretary. The prospectus modestly asserts "that this company, destined to be of the greatest use to property, has begun operations under the management of Mr. J. H. Fontagnene, with the assistance, and subject to control of a board of directors composed of nine members chosen from associate members and elected every six months, the office being gratuitous. * * * The greatest prudence and economy shall be the invariable rule of the company, which with some important improvements dictated by experience, is managed according to the principle of the American, French and English Companies.

Premiums on Common Risks.

Brick Building. Six months 3½ per cent per month; one, two and three years, 6, 5 and 4 per cent per month.

Frame Building. One year 1½ per cent per month, two and three years 1¼ and 1 per cent per month.

Office Bartlett St. No. 9.
In Jackson between Kearney and Dupont."

In spite of the "prudence and economy" and the four per cent per month on brick buildings, the fates were against this child of the now notorious Bartlett Alley (Chinatown), and it disappeared after a brief career as did many others of the same stripe.

A species of insurance was also carried on by the private bankers of the city at that time, as the following advertisement of Adams & Co. (selected from a number of similar purport) published early in the year 1852 shows.

"We have made arrangements for insurance to the extent of one million dollars on any one shipment, and are empowered to insure for other parties on gold dust, bars, coin and merchandise to and from New York and this city by endorsement on bills of lading at time of shipment."

By 1854 or 1855 the ephemeral companies were supplanted by sound eastern and foreign institutions, and the banks were confining their operations to legitimate channels.

All the solid companies were members of a Board of Fire Underwriters, and were bound to charge and *did* honestly charge rates of premium according to the following simple tariff.

1st Class—Building of brick; walls not less than 16 inches; fire walls 3 feet or over; roof of brick, earth, or metal; all openings protected by iron coverings; occupation non-hazardous; no frame exposure. On building, 2 per cent.; on merchandise, 2½ per cent.

2d Class—Building of brick; but deficient in any of the foregoing specifications; occupation non-hazardous; no frame exposure. On building, 2½ per cent.; on merchandise, 3 per cent.

3d Class—Building 2d class; with frame exposure. On building, 3 per cent.; on merchandise, 3½ per cent.

4th Class—Frame dwellings; plastered, with brick chimneys, and no frame exposure within 150 feet, 3½ per cent.

Hardly any other description of risk than those above described was deemed insurable until 1858, when opposition compelled the extension of the business.

When we consider that there were no brokers or brokerages, in those days, and only ten per cent. commissions paid to agents, that San Francisco, Sacramento, Stockton, San Jose and Oroville were rapidly building up with solid brick stores and hotels, that fires in these buildings were very rare—there being as yet no moral risk, for every one was making money—that there were hundreds of good detached frame risks which the companies refused altogether, it may be seen what a field was here for competition. Two men undertook to enter it.

One of these was Jonathan Hunt; the other was C. T. Hopkins.

CHAPTER II.

IN THE autumn of 1855 Messrs. Hunt and Hopkins, each unknown to the other, left San Francisco for New York, for the purpose of procuring the agencies of American companies for California. Mr. Hunt was an experienced New York merchant, then about 50 years old. He had visited San Francisco that year for the first time, to look about for a new field of labor, and being well acquainted in New York, had no trouble in securing the agencies of the Home, Niagara, Park, and three other good companies. Mr. Hopkins was then 29 years old and had been on the Coast since June, 1849. He had been for three years a clerk in the Custom House; one year master of a schooner, and for three years had led the adventurous and changeful life common to the Argonauts. He was a man of liberal education and of many trades. But all this did not help him to obtain insurance agencies. He then knew nothing about the business, and was not acquainted in New York. He could secure only the Lafarge, a small company of $150,000 capital, and the *correspondence* of five others, which agreed to take risks in New York on such of his applications as they might approve, and to pay losses when and how they might make it convenient. Of course this method would not work when it took 60 days to hear from an application, and in competition with the heavy English companies which issued policies and paid losses on the spot. But very few of the New York offices at that time believed in agency work at all. What they wanted was strictly local business. Conflagrations had not yet taught them to scatter their risks.

"What sir!" exclaimed James Lorimer Graham (then President of the Metropolitan Insurance Company, with $300,000 capital), when Mr. Hopkins applied for the full agency of his company. "What, sir! give *you* the whole benefit of our entire capital! Monstrous!"

Returning to San Francisco in January, 1856, with such widely differing equipments, neither of these gentlemen accomplished anything in the way of competition with the monopoly. Mr. Hunt at once joined the "ring" and built up a business sufficient to support his family for a year or two, and Mr. Hopkins shortly resigned his long-handled correspondence to take the sub-agency of the Liverpool and London, for Sacramento, Marysville and Oroville, where, by hard work and unremitting canvassing, he succeeding in collecting a premium income of about $20,000 per annum, for two years, every dollar of which was remitted to the company as fast as it came in. At the end of that time he returned to San Francisco where a much larger field was awaiting him, and Mr. Haven appointed as his successor, R. H. Stanley, a lawyer, who within the year absconded to the Sandwich Islands with several thousand dollars of the company's funds and a further large sum belonging to his clients. He was nevertheless appointed by the King, Attorney-General of the Islands, which office he held till his death.

Meantime the monopoly in fire insurance continued. The year 1856 was signalized by the celebrated Vigilance Committee, one of the results being to take Mr. Hunt out of the insurance business for a while. He was elected Tax Collector by the Peoples' Party in 1857, and his agencies passed into the hands of George S. Lambert.

In 1857 a curious fraud was successfully perpetrated in fire insurance by that celebrated adventurer Curtis L. North, a man whose career of ingenious rascality made him famous in several Eastern cities as well as in San Francisco. This man forged a power of attorney from the old United States Fire Insurance Company of New York, (Capital $250,000, and which never employed agents) in favor of two young men by name Chester and Sprague. He also procured the printing of policies, cards, stationery, &c., in their names as agents, in which the capital of the company was stated at $2,500,000, and being all ready, he flooded the town with advertisements the day after the steamer sailed, calculating to rake in a fine harvest of premiums during the eighty-five days that must elapse before the company could be heard from. For in those times the bi-monthly steamer was the only means of communication between New York and San Francisco. "Opposition to monopoly" was the trump card in this game. North, who was one of the best "canvassers" who ever took the street, worked like a beaver. Any risk was acceptable. Policies for $20,000 and $30,000 were freely written at half board rates, or at any price provided the cash were paid on the nail. The old underwriters were staggered by this unexpected blow. They knew it must be a fraud but could not prove it till the company in New York could be heard from. How much North profited by his bold scheme, no one but himself ever knew, but on the day before the arrival of the steamer that was expected to bring exposure, the office was closed, the books and blanks were thrown into the bay, and Chester and Sprague disappeared. An indignation meeting of the victims was called and numerously attended, but no recovery or arrest followed. North loudly protested his innocence, claiming that the fraud was entirely the work of the absconding agents, for whom he had only been working on commission, and who had deceived him worse than they had any one else. He was therefore not molested, and succeeded afterwards in heavily swindling a dry goods house before he left for New Orleans.

Meantime the days of monopoly in fire insurance were drawing to a close. In 1857, Edward McLean, a native of Connecticut, who had been a street contractor in San Francisco, and Treasurer of the old College of California (where he became intimate with Rev. Horace D. Bushnell, of Hartford, the then President of the college,) returned on a visit to Hartford. There his friend, Dr. Bushnell, procured for him the full agencies for California of the Hartford Fire Insurance Company, capital $400,000; the Phœnix, capital $200,000, and the Merchants', capital $200,000. Armed with these he repaired to Philadelphia, where he procured the Quaker City, fire and marine, whose advertised capital was $300,000, but was really nothing though McLean did not know it. At that time there was no State supervision over insurance companies in Pennsylvania, and while some of the best companies had grown up in Philadelphia, that city was also the favorite haunt of "wild cats." With these four agencies McLean returned to San Francisco, and undertook to do business. But being totally inexperienced, he shortly took into partnership John Fowler, an ex-clerk in Wells, Fargo & Co.'s Express, who had served several years as clerk in an insurance office in Rochester, N. Y. Fowler was of English birth, a good office man, but pompous and dictatorial in his manner, and though ambitious and anxious to do business, was above canvassing for it. So he brought no accession of custom to the firm. After six months of idle waiting for patrons who failed to appear, McLean & Fowler offered Hopkins a third interest in their concern, in consideration of his devoting his whole time to their interests. Hopkins accepted the offer, and thereupon the business began to move forward. The new firm being "outside the Board," whose lofty scale of rates and limited ideas of risks, offered a splendid opportunity to competitors, liberal advertising and hard work soon began to tell on the prejudices of the public, which had been heretofore in favor of English companies. The premiums were $5,000 the first month, $7,500 the second, $10,000 the third; in six months they reached $15,000. The firm then began to do marine business also for the Quaker City. Having no competitor at all in the field and plenty of risks offering on both hulls and cargo in the flourishing coastwise and Island trades, the premiums in this department soon reached $10,000 per month. Mr. Hopkins being familiar with shipping, made this his specialty, and made all the surveys himself. More facilities being now required, Fowler went East to procure them, and remained absent on this errand fourteen months.

He obtained some good fire companies, such as the Girard of Philadelphia, the Goodhue, the Metropolitan, and the Corn Exchange of New York, and the City Fire, of Hartford, though these were all small. But he failed to find out from its astute Secretary, H. R. Coggeshall, or from others, that the Quaker City was a first-class fraud, and he took on four other failing or fraudulent marine companies, the Great Western, the Washington and the Neptune of Philadelphia, and the Anchor, of New York.

Meantime the business in San Francisco was steadily growing. Hopkins made a tour through the State appointing some sixteen sub-agencies, this being the pioneer "special" work done in California. Among these agents were I. G. Wickersham at Petaluma, W. G. English at Sacramento, John Arnold at Placerville, C. F. Reed at San Jose, and others, many of whom were long identified with the insurance business. The premiums now rose to $30,000 per month and upwards. The office was enlarged by the occupation of the whole second floor of the building, N. E. corner of Clay and Battery streets, and more clerks were employed. Losses had thus far been light. Such as had occurred were promptly and liberally settled. A large amount of property, principally dwellings, hitherto deemed uninsurable, was covered. The rates and rules of the monopoly were relaxed. Insurance became popular everywhere. Other offices were established. The Hamburg-Bremen, Morris Speyer agent, made its appearance in 1858, and did a good business from the start. The New England Fire and Marine of Hartford, Wm. Faulkner agent, was also active. The old Ætna, E. H. Parker agent, commenced in 1858, but always followed a conservative course. Henceforth the insurance business was destined to be worked on the plane of other industries and to protect them all, on terms which all could afford to pay as in the older States.

On Fowler's return from his long absence in the fall of 1859, the firm was at the full tide of prosperity, its business aggregating at least three times that of any other office in the city, and resulting in large profit to the companies. But differences of opinions as to its management arose between the partners, which culminated in the withdrawal of Mr. Hopkins. Within a year afterwards

> "Unmerciful disaster
> Followed fast and followed faster."

The Philadelphia companies all failed, leaving large obligations unprotected. The losses of the other companies greatly increased. The firm became unpopular. Expenses multiplied. The good companies all withdrew. By the summer of 1861, the business was scattered and the firm dissolved. McLean went to Virginia City where he engaged in mining, and Fowler left the city.

About the same time the agency office of Richard S. Haven came to grief by the failure of his principal company, the Provincial, of Toronto. He shortly afterwards moved to Boston, where he organized the Boston Lloyds, which he managed as its attorney for several years. But this also finally failed, entailing a heavy loss to the subscribers. He died soon after.

Among the new fire agencies started during the palmy days of McLean & Fowler, was that of the Unity Fire Association, of England, Dickson, De Wolf & Co. agents. It was not a strong company, and did but little business in San Francisco. It disappeared in a year or two.

Thos. N. Cazneau made his appearance in San Francisco about 1858. He was an Irishman by birth, a small, wiry, indefatigable man, with a remarkably homely face, straight black hair, green eyes, and a most voluble tongue. His manners were charming, his tact almost proverbial, in fact, he was a born politician. His only principle was the expediency of the moment. Like J. P. Haven he was fond of the militia, and attained the rank of Brigadier-General in that service. He was a strong Democrat, and high in the counsels of that party, being Chairman of its State Committee during the Civil War. As a marine adjuster, he had enjoyed a high reputation in New Orleans for many years, and must have been about sixty years old when he first commenced practice in San Francisco. In point of skill in his profession he ranked with the celebrated General Tyler, of Boston, and his name on the Pacific soon became a terror to underwriters, unless he was employed in their interest. He deemed himself to be the attorney of the party employing him; not a judge or referee between the parties, which is the traditional attitude of an adjuster. When engaged by the consignee in a general average case, it was astonishing how many commissions would appear to be due his client; but if in the next case the insurer hired him, it was equally wonderful how few commissions were due. Mr. Cazneau became a power in the adjusting business strong enough to compel the Underwriters, a few years later, to combine against him for their own protection, at least to the extent of formulating "Rules and Customs in Marine Insurance," which clearly defined the points which he desired should remain uncertain so that he could continue to play with them for his own interest. Indeed, in one English general average he so perverted law and custom in favor of the claimants, that the English underwriters printed the statement and sent it to every marine insurance company in the world. They also sent to San Francisco for his portrait, intending to engrave that as frontispiece to the statement, but it was not to be had! The General was not given to admiring the sight of his own face, and his photographs were not in circulation. He died about 1872.

Another prominent character in marine insurance circles was Captain John C. Hoyt, the first resident agent at San Francisco of the New York Underwriters. Captain Hoyt was sent here in that capacity. He was a thoroughly honest and good man, and therefore disqualified to ferret out and defeat the numerous and ingenious devices of those rascally importers who regularly added large sums to their profits by successful frauds on underwriters. During his administration he approved claims in particular average amounting to about half a million annually, a sum, which under the more stringent rule of his successor in 1861, Captain Artemus T. Fletcher, shrunk to a tenth of that amount. But every one loved the kind-hearted and benevolent Captain Hoyt. He died in 1860, universally lamented.

About 1858 a small mutual fire insurance company was formed in San Francisco under the title of the German Mutual Fire Insurance Company. It had no capital, and was organized on the old country plan of paying losses by assessments. Its business was strictly limited to stores and dwellings owned by Germans, and it issued but a few hundred policies. It was wound up by the first Insurance Commissioner for lack of capital. As it was not designed for general business and its existence was hardly known beyond the circle of its few patrons, it was only nominally the pioneer of the local insurance interest.

CHAPTER III.

IT SEEMS in the light of the present day an astonishing fact, that the fleet of aged, storm-beaten craft, that had ploughed the seas for decades of years, should have so wonderfully survived the ocean tempests and the dangers of Cape Horn in 1849 and reached San Francisco in generally good condition. The probable reason for the exceptional good luck that attended the fleet that bore the "Argonauts," is found in the notably fine weather that was experienced in that year off Cape Horn, and also in the fact that few if any of the vessels were heavily laden, being for the most part filled up with passengers and their outfits; in fact, being in good sailing trim, or in sailor parlance "flying light."

Upon entering the Golden Gate before a fine breeze, and passing rapidly up the harbor of San Francisco on June 30, 1849, the first object that attracted attention was a stranded ship—she lay upon the sand bank or shoal that existed where Meigg's wharf is now built. The good ship Tahmaroo in her haste to reach her anchorage, had shaved the shore a little too closely, and found herself hard and fast. She was finally rescued by means of lightening her of cargo, and by the use of empty casks.

San Francisco harbor was then but little understood, the regular sea charts alone giving slender information; to keep in mid-channel and heave the lead was the only recourse, till in due time pilots made their appearance, supposed to have carefully studied out the dangers that existed.

It is the custom to give, to what were before unknown obstructions the name of the vessel that makes the discovery. Thus *Southampton Shoal* is known as the spot upon which the United States store ship Southampton stopped awhile. *Anita Rock*, just inside Fort Point, and now distinguished by a gridiron beacon, is the rock upon which the United States Quartermasters bark Anita met her fate. *Noonday Rock*, near Farralones, was discovered by the clipper ship Noonday, which rushed upon it at a speed of ten miles an hour, and sunk shortly after. *Blossom Rock* in the harbor, brought up the good ship Blossom. *Tonquin Shoal*, off Black Point, checked the onward career of the clipper ship Tonquin lumber laden, and hurrying on to dispose of her cargo at some hundreds of dollars per thousand feet in 1849. The ship was a total loss, but most of the cargo was saved. *Carrier Pigeon Point*, now called Pigeon Point for brevity's sake, saw the wreck of the new clipper Carrier Pigeon, on her first voyage from Boston in 1853. *Tennessee Cove*, a little north of Point Bonita, was the final resting place of the Panama steamer Tennessee, crowded with passengers from Panama, in 1855.

Wrecking in early days was attended with many drawbacks, for the want of good tugboats and wrecking apparatus, and most of the unfortunates that stranded proved a total loss. The wreck of the Carrier Pigeon was one of the most serious that had happened up to that time (1853.) The ship seemed to have gone straight to her destruction, running high and dry upon the beach, just inside of the point that now bears her name. The weather was fine, with the exception of a little fog, and it seemed as if some mistake of the bay had been made for that of San Francisco. The news of the wreck having been sent to the Boston agent of Underwriters in San Francisco, the steamer Sea Bird was chartered (besides some sailing vessels to follow after), to go to the scene of the wreck. Great was the desire to go down on the steamer, but the ubiquitous reporter, however, was not so conspicuous as would be the case to-day. Tom Batelle, a well known "sport" of those times, begged hard to be be permitted to go, but the agent utterly refused to load his steamer with dead heads, and sternly declined to take any one, except he went in some *official capacity*. Poor Tom was in a quandary, but was bound to go, and offered himself in an *official capacity* as Bottomry Bond, Esq., or General Average. He went. Captain Bob Waterman was employed as the stevedore of the wrecking crew on board the Sea Bird, and upon arriving at the wreck found the ship lying in an easy position in the bay, and the crew impatiently awaiting the arrival of a steamer which should convey them to San Francisco. Upon seeing Captain Bob they declined to work. Calculating upon the aid of the ship's crew, no very large independent force had been taken on the steamer, and trouble seemed brewing. It was of no use, the crew would not listen to reason; the spokesman said, "Oh we know you too well, Bully Waterman, and we propose to let others do the work while *you* are boss." Captain Bob was equal to the occasion, and told the rebellious crew that they would be landed on the beach, and not a man would be allowed to leave on the steamer, unless he aided in loading her. The distance by land to San Francisco was about sixty miles, across a desolate country with no road except it might be a single trail, and horses and mules scarce and dear. Of course, the crowd concluded to go to work. That night the Sea Bird, lying uneasily at anchor in a seaway, brought her chain across her bow, and twisted her fore-foot, causing a bad leak. So serious was it that after getting started for San Francisco, it was found the water gained rapidly, and she was therefore turned about and finally beached below Point Ano Nueva (New Year), the water putting out her fires just as her keel grated upon the sands. She was filled with cargo from the ship, and to enable her to keep up a head of steam, boxes of boots and shoes, casks of hams, and combustible freight generally, was used to feed the fires. The agent was landed together with a son of the steamer's owner (Bully Wright, as he was called), and proceeded to San Francisco for assistance, with twelve horses driven ahead for changes, and a vaquero guide. They reached San Francisco at 11 o'clock at night, and before daylight next morning went outside the Heads on the steamer Goliah, on their return to the wreck, and with no public information given of their visit.

On the trip across the country the route seemed lined with "beach-combers" from San Francisco, going to the scene of disaster for plunder.

Considerable cargo went ashore at the Cove and was gathered up by these men, and in the settlement of salvage claims much annoyance was experienced. It was agreed that the stranding of the Sea Bird was not to be made public in San Francisco, but on the day succeeding the arrival of the messengers, a considerable amount (risk) on the Sea Bird was taken by one of our insurance companies, the owner averring he was somewhat alarmed at her long absence. After the lapse of a few days the Goliah returned with a portion of the wrecked cargo, and of course the condition of the Sea Bird was soon known. The insurance company repudiated, and a law suit was the result. It was won by the defendants, the court deciding that it was proved that parties from the wreck had visited San Francisco at the time of the disaster, leaving again quite secretly, and it was therefore possible that plaintiffs had some inkling, if not more, of the disaster. The Sea Bird was rescued after lying nearly six months on the beach, and did good service for years after, being finally burned at Puget Sound.

Fort Point has proved a veritable graveyard for ships, some twelve vessels having stranded there, some seven or eight of them a total loss. Six ships have struck on Mile Rocks, and many of them seriously damaged. The Sea Nymph stranded at Point Reyes, the result of it being a total loss amounting to $300,000. Eleven ships have struck on Alcatraz, and rocks in that vicinity, notably Arch Rock.

In 1862, the ship Flying Dragon, after a very short passage from Australia, coal laden, struck on Arch Rock in a fog, with a pilot on board, and became a total loss. The ship was visited at once by J. S. Bacon, agent of Underwriters, with a tug boat, which returned again to the city front for help to rescue the vessel. Upon her way back to the ship, the tug boat met the ship's boat with the captain and part of the crew, and a mattress spread across, on which was a litter of pigs. Bacon hailed the boat with:

"Well, Captain, has the good ship gone?"

"Aye, aye, sir," says Captain Watson," but I have saved *my Bacon.*"

Captain Watson is now a Marine Surveyor in San Francisco. There was one curious fact in connection with this wreck. The ship careened over and went down in deep water alongside the rock, at the change of tide she rose on her keel, and toppled over to starboard, and sank to be seen no more.

In 1863, the ship Aquilla arrived with the materials and armament of the monitor Comanche on board, a very heavy cargo. The monitor was to be set up in San Francisco. The ship lay at a wharf somewhere near the spot now occupied by Hathaway's wharf, and grounding on a ledge of rock alongside the wharf, she bilged and went down bow foremost at high water.

The wrecking of that ship is a matter of curious history. It was an expensive undertaking, but city and State loaned money for the purpose of recovering the monitor, and the Comanche was finally built and launched from the beach near the Aquilla. The ship was also finally raised, and repaired.

In 1862, the ship Polynesia (in ballast) took fire while lying at anchor in the harbor, and while burning furiously was taken in tow by a stern-wheel steamer, commanded by a Captain Trueworthy, and towed through the fleet lying at anchor, at the imminent peril of the vessels around. Nothing else could be done to save her, and it was feared she would set fire to the sails and tarred rigging of other vessels, and towing was decided upon. Captain Trueworthy performed the duty in a masterly manner, amid cheers from people assembled on the docks; she was beached at the South bay, where she soon burned to the water's edge. There was no steam captain that was willing to undertake the job of towing till Trueworthy volunteered. It was considered a fool-hardy undertaking, but there is "nothing so successful as success."

As has been before remarked, tug boats were unknown in early times, and even after their advent the towing tariff was so exorbitant that few ship masters were disposed to use them, and large ships continued to beat out of the harbor in going to sea, an operation attended with considerable danger on account of the necessity of approaching near the land on either side. Tacking to and fro, and the wind dying out or baffling, placed a ship in a dangerous position. Many accidents happened at Fort Point and Mile Rocks, by ships caught in the eddies and all control of them lost. The ship Radiant in a fine day was stranded on Angel Island, swept ashore by the current while in stays; she was rescued at high water. A tug had been sent to her, but the ship was afloat before the tug arrived; a dispute on this point caused litigation and hard feeling against the tugs.

The danger attendant upon handling a large ship tacking on a lee shore, made it apparent that towing was the safer plan, and the Boston agent of Underwriters after long effort, succeeded in securing written permission from the Board, allowing ships insured there "to go to sea without pilots, when in tow of a competent tug." Towage and pilotage together, was an onerous tax on vessels, and ship masters were unwilling to assume it. Ships must have pilots to comply with the insurance clause, but after the introduction of the above mentioned permit, towing to sea has been generally practiced, till at the present day it is universal, the pilots and tug boats joining hands in the business.

The remains of the Italian bark Brignadello, laden with marble and other merchandise, stranded in 1868 upon the beach south of the Cliff House were visible for many years after. The ship Patrician in going over the bar deeply laden, struck, as was supposed at the time, a sunken wreck, but no wreck was known in such a position, and it is probable she was out of the channel. She had no pilot on board and was run upon what is known as the "potato patch," and *remained there*.

The Farralones have been the graveyard of two vessels laden with valuable cargoes, only a small portion of which was saved.

Ship Bengal laden with lumber from the North, and bound to Callao, struck on a rock near Point Reyes and carried away her rudder and opened the seams about the stern post. She was brought to San Francisco, and the expense of discharging and repairs being serious, a coffer-dam was built at the suggestion of a leading ship carpenter, the first attempt of the kind. Dry-docks and ship carpenters predicted a failure, but the repairs were successfully made, and the great expense avoided.

Prior to the building of the dry-dock at Hunter's Point in 1868, ships were compelled to make use of the floating dock at Mare Island, entailing heavy towing charges up and down, and a deal of red tape at the Island. The building of the Hunter's Point dock was therefore hailed with great joy by masters and underwriters.

Many pages might be written respecting shipping disasters of the earlier times, but we have introduced only a few of the most noted. At the present day San Francisco is as well supplied with all that is required for wrecking purposes as the Eastern cities, and if the situation and elements permit, ships are rarely totally lost.

Puget Sound, and the Straits of Fuca, are now monopolizing the wrecks, the heavily laden coal ships that have been obliged to succumb to the heavy winter weather around the straits, are getting to be somewhat numerous, and teach a lesson in lading of vessels, that may perhaps be heeded, but the greed of shipowners is an obstacle.

A word might be said respecting the faithful old servants that still live to do duty on the seas. Very many ships it is well known made their last voyage when they arrived at this port in 1849. Worn out and rheumatic, they were patched up for the voyage, and favored by good weather arrived here at last to lay their bones. Converted into warehouses, lodging-houses, steamboat landings, &c., they have at last succumbed to inevitable decay.

And yet some "old timers," are now on the ocean wave. The bark Coral, of the whaling fleet, has seen her threescore years and ten, and is still hunting whales. The bark Amethyst (lost a year ago in the Arctic) had completed her threescore year and five. Schooner Page, now at anchor in our harbor, was once a dandy packet, and known as a fast vessel, plying between Boston and New York; she is still doing duty at an age of fifty-seven years. Ship Coquimbo, brings her regular cargoes of lumber from Puget Sound, aged forty-seven years; she was built for the trade between Boston and Valparaiso. She was a very large vessel for those times (850 tons), and has done good service for nearly half a century. She has been ashore at Puget Sound once, was rescued and repaired, and except a little curvature of the spine, looks to be all in the fashion, with her antique model, and sort of Mother Hubbard style. Forty-five years ago the bark Stamboul was one of the Mediterranean clippers engaged in the fruit trade, a vessel whose early beauty and style attracted thousands of sea lovers whenever she arrived. She is now chasing whales, and has reached the last occupation the old timers are wont to follow, viz.: that of hunting for "ile and bone."

The Marine Underwriting department in the history of California will some day fill a volume of no small dimensions, and be full of interest. It is a little history of itself.

Board of Marine Underwriters.

IN 1864 the agents and officers of several marine insurance companies, and marine underwriters doing business in this city, pledged themselves to adhere to certain rates of premiums and rules of marine insurance. This practically organized the Board of Marine Underwriters. The tariff went into operation February 1st, 1864, and the pledge was signed by the following gentlemen:

D. C. McRuer, President, C. T. Hopkins, Secretary, for the California Mutual Insurance Company; James P. Flint, President, J. B. Scotchler, Secretary, for the Merchants' Mutual Marine Insurance Company; Janson, Bond & Co., for the Washington, Metropolitan and Pacific Mutual Insurance Companies of New York; C. Adolphe Low & Co., holders of New York open policies; Falkner, Bell & Co., for London Lloyds; Gustave Touchard, Secretary for the Assurers' underwriting at the California Lloyds; Koopmanschap & Co., Agents for the North China Insurance Company; Lazard Freres, Agents of Atlantic Mutual Insurance Company, New York.

This arrangement held in force until 1865, when at a meeting held August 25th a constitution and by-laws were adopted, and the name "The Board of Marine Underwriters of San Francisco" was chosen. The members of the Board and the companies represented were as follows:

Gustave Touchard, California Lloyds; C. Adolphe Low & Co., New York Underwriters; Falkner, Bell & Co., British and Foreign Marine Insurance Company; Jonathan Hunt, President, A. J. Ralston, Secretary, Pacific Insurance Company; Bigelow & Bro., Home Insurance Company, New York, Security Insurance Company, New York, Phenix Insurance Company, New York; Lazard Freres, Atlantic Mutual Insurance Company, New York; Wm. Holdridge, President, W. H. Stevens, Secretary, Home Mutual Insurance Company; Albert Miller, President, C. T. Hopkins, Secretary, California Insurance Company; C. L. Taylor, Vice-President, J. B. Scotchler, Secretary, Merchants' Mutual Marine Insurance Company; A. T. Fletcher, New York Board Underwriters; J. S. Bacon, Boston Board Underwriters; Jas. de Fremery, Amsterdam Board Underwriters; Gustavus Zeil, Bremen Board Underwriters; Koopmanschap & Co., North China Insurance Company; J. E. René French Underwriters. The officers of the Board that year were James P. Flint, President; Gustave Touchard Vice-President; C. T. Hopkins, Secretary; J. B. Scotchler, Treasurer. The work performed by the Board was of great benefit to the marine business of the port. A tariff was adopted and a form of marine policy, which all companies used for many years. Mr. Hopkins, the secretary, who remained in office twenty years, originated the *Wreck Register*, an annual compilation of all marine losses, showing the voyages and the average loss on each voyage as compared with the current rates of premium. These statistics proved of the greatest value at the time, and are still not only of use to underwriters, but are of great interest to all who have a fondness for the maritime history, as they contain the list of all the famous vessels in the Pacific Coast trade lost during those years. That published for the period covering 1861-66, just after the war was ended, contains information, so worded it will create a smile now that war issues are dead, and the friendship between the North and South once more cemented. We give the extract verbatim.

"The following captures of whalemen were made during 1865, in the Pacific and Arctic Oceans, by the British pirate Shenandoah or Sea King. Of these, only three, viz.: the W. C. Nye, Edward Carey and Susan Abigail, were owned in San Francisco.

April 1	Edward Carey	Ascension Island	Burned.
April 1	Harvest (Hawaiian)	" "	"
April 1	Pearl	" "	"
April 1	Hester	" "	"
May 27	Abigail	Gulf of Amur	"
June 21	Euphrates	Behring Sea	"
June 22	Wm. Thompson	" "	"
June 22	Jireh Swift	" "	"
June 23	Susan Abigail	" "	"
June 25	Gen. Williams	" "	"
June 26	Nimrod	" "	"
June 26	W. C. Nye	" "	"
June 26	Catharine	" "	"
June 27	Gipsy	" "	"
June 27	Isabella	" "	"
June 28	Hillman	" "	"
June 28	J. Howland	" "	"
June 28	Nassau	" "	"
June 28	Brunswick	" "	"
June 28	Waverly	" "	"
June 28	Martha 2nd	" "	"
June 28	Congress	" "	"
June 28	Favorite	" "	"
June 28	Covington	" "	"
June 28	Milo	" "	Bonded
June 27	General Pike	" "	"
June 28	Nile	" "	"
June 28	James Maury	" "	"

In 1881 new energy was given the Board by a partial revision of its constitution and by-laws, and it now regulates the marine business of the whole Pacific Coast shipping, having special agents at all important points where ships or cargoes are insured by San Francisco offices. In 1885 Mr. Hopkins retired from active business and Edm. L. Woods, the present Secretary, was elected to succeed him. Gustave Touchard, first vice President of the Association, was elected President January 8, 1866, and Col. C. L. Taylor, another veteran underwriter was elected vice President at the same time. Mr. Touchard has continued to hold office, having been annually re-elected since that date.

Board of Marine Underwriters.

Mr. Touchard's long connection with the Board as vice-president and president, not only is a proof of his great popularity in the profession generally, but a tribute to his ability in marine underwriting, with which profession he has been so prominently identified. On February 17th, 1887, he was unanimously elected an honorary member of the Association of Marine Underwriters. On that occasion Mr. Touchard's long and honorable career, his friendship for young men, his high qualities as an underwriter, were eloquently referred to in speeches, and the action of the Association was conveyed to him in a most complimentary letter.

Col. Taylor is a native of Maine and came to California in the spring of 1850. His first business venture on this Coast was in co-partnership with J. E. Blethen in the building material trade, from which he retired to join J. B. Swasey, of Boston, in the shipping and commission business. This firm had headquarters in Boston and San Francisco and for many years transacted a flourishing trade. Col. Taylor has occupied many positions of trust and honor in this State, and is universally regarded as one of the most progressive business men and an accomplished underwriter. He is now president of the Sun Insurance Company and still conducts his commission business. His connection with underwriting has been long and honorable and in its marine branch he has ever been active, well posted and reliable. Col. Taylor resigned from the Board in 1878, temporarily retiring from insurance business; but on re-entering the field a year or two later, again joined the Board, and at its first annual election thereafter, he was unanimously elected vice-president, and still holds that position. Edm. L. Woods was vice-president during the interim. At present all marine companies doing business in San Francisco are represented in the Board.

Association of Marine Underwriters.

WAS organized December 17, 1885, the projector of the Association being Frederick S. Butler, of the Union Insurance Company, at whose residence the preliminary meeting was held. The charter members of the association were F. S. Butler, N. T. James, Edm. L. Woods, W. H. C. Fowler, C. J. Okell, H. H. Nagle, J. G. Lucas, Chas. C. Thorn, H. S. Smith and J. B. Levison. The object of the association, as stated in its by-laws, are to promote harmony and good practice in the profession, the interchange of views, opinions and personal experience, the discussion of topics of interest to the profession and the consideration of such subjects as may be brought before the association. The association is at present engaged in collecting valuable statistical and other information in reference to all the ports of the Pacific Coast, including those of British Columbia and Alaska. The information, when completed, will be of special value to underwriters and shippers, and will probably be published by the association.

It is the intent and purpose of the association to take an active interest in all matters bearing upon marine underwriting, particularly in reference to policies, risks and rates. It will be a mistake to suppose that the association merely aims at acquiring information. Its settled plan is to make practical use of its acquirements in regulating the marine business of the Coast, by an effort to place rate and risk on all fours.

The procedure is unique. Monthly meetings are held, at which papers prepared by different members are read, after which general discussion and criticism is in order. These papers are preserved, and at the end of the year are printed in pamphlet form for distribution among members and friends. A correspondence is maintained, also, with kindred associations in London, Liverpool, New York, Australia, New Zealand and other sections, through which channels much valuable information is obtained, and disseminated. It will be seen that the principal object is to acquire a knowledge of the profession that could not be obtained by individual effort. The membership differs from that of the Marine Board of Underwriters in that each member of the association has a vote which is not affected by a change of company or by the fact that several members belong to the same company, while in the board each company has but one vote and but one member of the company can represent it in the board.

The social features of the association are not neglected, as in addition to the cultivation of friendship which naturally comes through the pleasant monthly debates and discussions, a semi-annual dinner materially assists in promoting good fellowship among the members.

The association commenced with eleven members, N. T. James, Marine Secretary of the Fireman's Fund Insurance Company, being elected first President of the organization, Edm. L. Woods, Vice-President; F. S. Butler, Secretary and

Association of Marine Underwriters.

WM. GREER HARRISON.

to the earnest efforts of these gentlemen much of the subsequent success of the association is due.

At the last annual election Wm. Greer Harrison, resident manager of the Thames & Mersey Marine Insurance Company, was elected president, and he has given the affairs of the association his careful attention. F. S. Butler of the Union Insurance Company, received the well merited position of Vice-President of the club, and H. Stephenson Smith, of the Sun Insurance Company, was elected Secretary.

The association, which now numbers thirty-four representative underwriters beside a number of honorary members, is steadily growing in the esteem of the profession and in membership. The full list is annexed :

Name.	*Company.*
N. T. James	Fireman's Fund
W. H. C. Fowler	California
F. S. Butler	Union
Edw. L. Woods	Maritime and Union
H. H. Nagle	Canton
J. G. Laws	——
J. B. Levison	Anglo-Nevada
H. Stephenson Smith	Sun
C. C. Thorne	Globe Marine
C. J. Okell	British American
W. J. Dutton	Fireman's Fund
H. Durbrow	London and Provincial
H. W. Sex	Swiss Marine
W. Greer Harrison	Thames and Mersey
Arthur Page	Union of Canton
J. L. Wood	Commercial Union
C. F. Mullins	Commercial Union
C. V. S. Gibbs	Adjuster
W. C. Gibbs	Adjuster
G. J. Ritter	Reliance
A. H. Small	British and Foreign
L. Rosenthal	Swiss Marine
J. L. Scotchler	Fireman's Fund
H. C. Havens	Fireman's Fund
W. W. Gollin	Transatlantic
C. P. Farnfield	Anglo-Nevada
W. S. Davis	Standard Marine
M. A. Newell	California
Chas. A. Laton	Commercial
Hugh Craig	New Zealand
G. Cottrell	Boston Marine
C. S. Spinney	Marine
F. G. Agnew	South British
George Steele	California

HONORARY MEMBERS:

W. A. Walker, Agent S. F. Board Marine Underwriters......New York
C. T. Hopkins, ex-President California Insurance Company.....Pasadena
Gustave Touchard, President Union Insurance Company...San Francisco
S. Cross, Underwriter Thames & Mersey Insurance Company.....Liverpool
Morris C. Bates, Editor Commercial News and Shipping List..San Francisco

The Insurance Commission.

THE causes that led to the creation of the Insurance Commission by the State are briefly referred to elsewhere. The number of irresponsible "wild cat" companies was on the increase and after much talk in the legislature the present law was approved in March, 1868. The office was opened on the 5th of May following, in the Fireman's Fund building where it has since remained. George W. Mowe was the first commissioner, with Andrew D. Smith as deputy.

M. M. RHORER.

J. W. Foard was the second commissioner, succeeding Mr. Mowe and taking possession of the office on April 1st, 1872. E. V. Thwing was his deputy up to the time of his death, when M. M. Rhorer was appointed by Mr. Foard on January 1st, 1876, and has been reappointed as deputy by the succeeding commissioners up to the present time. Mr. Rhorer, whose picture is given here, has been so long in office and has proved such an efficient officer, courteous and obliging, without, however, losing sight of the special duties assigned to him, that he has the warm friendship of all the profession, and his thorough knowledge of the workings of the office makes him an invaluable assistant to the commissioner.

Mr. Foard's term of office expired on April 8th, 1878, when he was succeeded by John C. Maynard. His successor was George A. Knight, who took possession of the office on May 1st, 1883, and his successor was the present commissioner, J. C. L. Wadsworth, who took possession on April 9th, 1886.

From the records of the commissioner's office the following statistics regarding both fire and marine insurance business of California have been compiled.

FIRE INSURANCE.

Year.	Amount Written.	Premiums on Same.	Losses Paid.	Ratio of Losses to Prem's.
1875	$221,653,672.00	$3,493,381.28	$ 987,968.57	28.3
1876	237,013,037.00	3,711,618.08	1,268,397.88	34.2
1877	256,893,278.00	3,933,920.02	1,219,966.08	31.0
1878	228,630,041.00	3,530,322.23	931,905.81	26.3
1879	228,964,600.00	3,433,004.15	1,116,292.88	32.5
1880	252,179,539.00	3,620,267.60	1,175,071.32	32.5
1881	261,342,913.00	3,812,436.49	1,268,911.23	33.3
1882	268,306,348.00	4,038,382.62	2,612,908.11	39.9
1883	278,872,257.00	4,191,820.96	1,629,818.56	39.1
1884	296,648,573.00	4,328,062.11	1,293,391.48	28.5
1885	282,011,385.00	4,580,881.39	2,053,357.05	44.8
1886	308,521,409.00	5,183,772.23	2,651,371.08	51.2

MARINE INSURANCE.

Year.	Amount Written.	Premiums on Same.	Losses Paid.	Ratio of Losses to Prem's.
1875	$ 71,164,714.00	$1,524,067.23	$ 781,612.79	51.1
1876	72,803,884.00	1,551,653.45	not reported	
1877	70,813,627.00	1,356,125.17	*436,709.52	
1878	77,106,770.00	1,363,331.61	*351,128.15	
1879	75,314,027.00	1,300,879.21	*361,163.80	
1880	82,650,210.00	1,242,500.03	620,362.34	49.9
1881	103,739,028.00	1,689,209.91	681,067.39	40.3
1882	113,323,785.00	1,819,086.16	1,127,271.25	62.2
1883	113,275,805.00	1,587,350.16	990,281.81	60.9
1884	110,287,744.00	1,133,138.20	368,110.86	32.7
1885	103,031,139.00	1,395,903.67	856,630.41	61.3
1886	120,900,347.00	1,545,270.79	674,925.29	43.8

* As far as reported.

The Insurance Commission.

The year of organization, location, name of President, Secretary, and Agent or Attorney for California, and date of certificate of authority issued by the Insurance Commissioner, and the date of commencement of business in California of all Insurance Companies authorized to transact business on December 31, 1886, is given in the annexed table:

Year of Organization	Name.	Location.	President.	Secretary.	Agent for California.	Date of Certificate Issued by Insurance Commissioner.	Commenced business in California.
1883	Anglo-Nevada	San Francisco	Louis Sloss	Z. P. Clark		Dec. 1, 1883	Dec. 1, 1883
1861	California	San Francisco	L. L. Bromwell	W. H. C. Fowler		June 14, 1868	February, 1861
1872	Commercial	San Francisco	John H. Wise	Chas. A. Laton		March 1, 1872	March 1, 1872
1863	Fireman's Fund	San Francisco	D. J. Staples	Wm. J. Dutton		June 24, 1868	June, 1863
1864	Home Mutual	San Francisco	J. F. Houghton	Chas. R. Story		June 24, 1868	Dec. 15, 1864
1869	Oakland Home	Oakland	Wm. P. Jones	Wm. F. Blood		Feb. 5, 1869	Feb. 5, 1869
1883	Southern California	Los Angeles	E. F. Spence	D. E. Miles		Feb. 28, 1883	Feb. 28, 1883
1872	State Investment	San Francisco	A. J. Bryant	Chas. H. Cushing		January 13, 1872	Jan. 13, 1872
1882	Sun	San Francisco	C. L. Taylor	E. E. Potter		Feb. 1, 1883	Feb. 1, 1882
1866	Union	San Francisco	Gustave Touchard	Jas. D. Bailey		June 25, 1868	June 20, 1866
1819	Ætna	Hartford	L. J. Hendee	J. Goodnow	G. C. Boardman	June 1868	June 20, 1863
1853	Agricultural	Watertown, N. Y.	J. M. Stebbins	H. M. Stevens	Hutchinson & Mann	August 2, 1876	Aug. 2, 1876
1824	Alliance Marine	London	Lord Rothschild	Douglas Owen	Parrott & Co.	May 28, 1880	May 28, 1880
1871	Amazon	Cincinnati	Gazzam Gano	J. H. Beattie	A. L. Bromwell	October 1, 1872	Oct. 1, 1872
1846	American	Newark	F. H. Harris	J. H. Worden	Balfour, Guthrie & Co.	August 13, 1883	Aug. 13, 1883
1853	American Central	St. Louis	Geo. T. Cram	C. Christensen	Stolp V. Watt	April 15, 1874	April 15, 1874
1810	American Fire	Philadelphia	T. H. Montgomery	R. Marsh	Brown, Craig & Co.	October 31, 1872	Oct. 31, 1872
1808	Atlas	London	Sir W. J. W. Baynes	W. J. Tickle	H. M. Newhall & Co.	August 13, 1885	Aug. 13, 1885
1864	Baloise	Basle, Switzerland	B. P. Vischer	C. Blaskarle	H. W. Sye	Nov. 29, 1876	Nov. 29, 1876
1873	Boston Marine	Boston	H. H. Folgers	Thos. H. Lord	J. N. Knowles	Aug. 22, 1882	Aug. 22, 1882
1872	Boylston	Boston	Jos. W. Balch	W. Glover	H. M. Newhall & Co.	Dec. 16, 1881	Dec. 16, 1881
1833	British America	Toronto	Jno. Morrison	Geo. E. Robbins	Cheli & Woolley	March 1, 1873	March 11, 1873
1863	British and Foreign Marine	Liverpool	Thos. Chilton	A. McNeill	Balfour, Guthrie & Co.	October 10, 1868	Aug. 25, 1864
1805	Caledonian	Edinburgh	D. Deuchar	D. J. Stevenson	Balfour, Guthrie & Co.	July 24, 1883	July 24, 1883
1835	Canton	Hong Kong	Jardine, Matheson & Co.		Parrott & Co.	June 1, 1882	June 1, 1882
1865	China Traders	Hong Kong	L. Poesnecker	A. S. Harlie	Williams, Dimond & Co.	Sept. 4, 1871	Sept. 4, 1871
1871	Chinese	Hong Kong		S. J. Gower	W. T. Coleman & Co.	June 9, 1877	June 9, 1873
1837	Citizens'	St. Louis	J. B. M. Kehlor	J. P. Harrison	Hutchinson & Mann	Sept. 5, 1878	Sept. 5, 1878
1836	Citizens'	New York	E. A. Walton	F. M. Parker	C. Bertheau	Nov. 27, 1868	Nov. 27, 1867
1845	City of London Fire	London	Sir H. E. Knight	J. C. Phillips	W. J. Callingham	May 19, 1881	May 19, 1881
1850	Clinton Fire	New York	C. J. Patterson, Jr.	C. E. W. Chambers	Jacobs & Easton	August 6, 1883	Aug. 6, 1883
1861	Commercial Union	London	Alfred Giles	A. A. Bennett	C. F. Mullins	June 22, 1870	June 22, 1870
1870	Concordia Fire	Milwaukee	J. H. Janssen	C. Wedsinger	Jacobs & Easton	April 22, 1886	April 22, 1886
1850	Connecticut Fire	Hartford	J. D. Browne	C. R. Burt	Webb, Dickson	August 20, 1875	Aug. 20, 1875
1850	Continental	New York	H. H. Lamport	Cyrus Peck	Hutchinson & Mann	Sept. 21, 1872	Sept. 21, 1872
1877	Eliot	Boston	W. C. George	A. P. Curtis	F. E. Potter	October 23, 1877	Oct. 23, 1877
1817	Fire Association of Philadelphia	Philadelphia	J. Leighton	W. S. Windrige	Chas. A. Laton	Dec. 8, 1879	Dec. 8, 1879
1844	Fire Insurance Association	London	P. Lock, Man'r in U. S.		Isaac & Dunn, W. L. Chalmers	Sept. 29, 1881	Sept. 29, 1881
1825	Fireman's	Baltimore	J. M. Anderson	W. Armstrong	Hutchinson & Mann	Nov. 21, 1881	Nov. 21, 1881
1855	Firemen's	Newark	S. R. W. Heath	C. Colyer	Hutchinson & Mann	June 2, 1882	June 2, 1882
1879	Fonciere	Paris	A. Fischstet	M. Rondler	Hutchinson & Mann	Nov. 20, 1880	Nov. 20, 1880
1829	Franklin Fire	Philadelphia	J. W. McAllister	E. T. Cresson	F. E. Potter	May 15, 1883	May 15, 1883
1879	Franco-Hungarian	Budapest	A. Moscovics	H. Brey	Gutte & Frank	Dec. 20, 1886	Dec. 20, 1886
1861	German	Freeport, Illinois	M. Bettinger	F. Gund	Jacobs & Easton	April 9, 1883	April 9, 1883
1872	German American	New York	E. Oelbermann	J. A. Silvey	Thos. C. Grant	October 10, 1872	Oct. 10, 1872
1859	Germania Fire	New York	R. Garrigue	H. Schlumann	Gutte & Frank	October 25, 1869	Oct. 25, 1869
1853	Girard Fire and Marine	Philadelphia	A. S. Gillett	E. F. Merrill	Hutchinson & Mann	Sept. 22, 1875	Sept. 22, 1875
1849	Glen's Falls	Glen's Falls, N. Y.	R. M. Little	J. L. Cunningham	Jacobs & Easton	April 8, 1886	April 8, 1886
1871	Globe Marine	London	R. Whitford	H. F. Cobb	W. L. Chalmers & Co.	Feb. 26, 1887	Feb. 26, 1887
1821	Guardian Fire and Life	London	H. G. Lubbock	T. J. C. Brown	W. J. Landers	October 21, 1876	Oct. 21, 1876
1854	Hamburg-Bremen	Hamburg	H. Moschmeyer	S. Von Seelen	Sayper & Bews	Sept. 21, 1882	May 1, 1867
1856	Hamburg-Magdeburg	Hamburg	A. Bredikow	T. Hagedorn	Gutte & Frank	August 16, 1876	Aug. 16, 1876
1852	Hanover Fire	New York	B. S. Walcott	J. Remsen Lane	C. Bertheau	October 23, 1880	Oct. 23, 1880
1810	Hartford Fire	Hartford	Geo. L. Chase	P. C. Royce	Belden & Cofran	January 17, 1870	Jan. 17, 1870
1858	Helvetia Marine	St. Gall, Switzerland	C. B. Jacob	M. T. Grossman	H. W. Sye	Nov. 28, 1876	Nov. 28, 1876
1861	Helvetia Swiss Fire	St. Gall, Switzerland	C. B. Jacob	M. T. Grossman	H. W. Sye	Dec. 6, 1876	Dec. 6, 1876
1853	Home	New York	C. J. Martin	J. H. Washburn	A. E. Magill	Nov. 13, 1869	Nov. 13, 1869
1857	Howard	New York	H. A. Oakley	C. A. Hull	Jacobs & Easton	July 30, 1883	July 30, 1883
1803	Imperial	London	C. Bastard	E. C. Smith	G. H. Peirce	Sept. 26, 1868	May 1, 1867
1794	Insurance Co. of North America	Philadelphia	Chas. Platt	G. E. Fryer	Thos. A. Mitchell	October 13, 1873	Oct. 13, 1873
1794	Ins. Co. of the State of Penn.	Philadelphia	Geo. G. Sternell	J. M. Hollingshead	Brown, Craig & Co.	Feb. 15, 1878	Feb. 15, 1878
1879	International Marine	Liverpool	T. H. Hayden	W. W. Clay	Donaldson & Co.	August 25, 1880	Aug. 25, 1880
1852	Lancashire	Manchester	N. Stelmerdine	Geo. Stewart	E. H. Carpenter	July 20, 1871	July 20, 1871
1879	Lion Fire	London	Ellis Elias	Thos. H. Bell	G. D. Dornin	April 12, 1880	April 12, 1880
1836	Liverpool and London and Globe	Liverpool	Jas. M. Dove	Alex. Duncan	Chas. D. Haven	Sept. 26, 1868	May 1, 1867
1720	London	London	L. A. Wallace	S. E. Lancaster	Webb, Dickson	August 28, 1872	Aug. 28, 1872
1861	London and Lancashire	Liverpool	C. G. Fothergill	G. H. Flood	Balfour, Guthrie & Co.	Nov. 6, 1879	Nov. 6, 1879
1862	London and Provincial Fire	London	F. C. Morgan	H. Williams	H. W. Sye	April 10, 1882	April 10, 1882
1868	London and Provincial Marine	London	J. Borradaile	A. J. Daniel	Hutchinson & Mann	April 3, 1878	April 3, 1878
1844	Magdeburg Fire	Magdeburg	R. Dubaszke	E. F. Sharake	Gutte & Frank	Sept. 6, 1886	Sept. 6, 1886
1872	Magdeburg General	Magdeburg		Th. Gessmann	Gutte & Frank	August 31, 1876	Aug. 31, 1876
1824	Manchester Fire	Manchester	J. B. Northcott	F. Hodson	Balfour, Guthrie & Co.	April 22, 1880	April 22, 1880
1870	Mannheim	Mannheim	F. Engelhorn	C. Gerlinger	Geo. Marcus & Co.	Nov. 19, 1881	Nov. 19, 1881
1870	Man On	Hong Kong	Quan Hoi Chuen	Wan Lin Yuen	Tuck, Chong & Co.	October 31, 1881	Oct. 31, 1881
1864	Maritime	Liverpool	J. B. Smith	R. A. Strickland	E. L. Woods	July 3, 1871	July 3, 1871
1858	Merchants'	Newark	Henry Powles	J. E. Mulliken	Jacobs & Easton	January 31, 1883	Jan. 31, 1883
1850	Merchants'	New York	F. H. Marsh	L. S. Mettler	Jacobs & Easton	May 8, 1884	May 8, 1884
1865	Merchants' Mutual	Baltimore	G. H. Miller	J. Wilson	Gray & [illegible]	July 23, 1886	July 23, 1886
1881	Michigan Fire and Marine	Detroit	D. M. Ferry	E. C. Preston	F. E. Potter	June 29, 1886	June 29, 1886
1822	National	Dublin		H. Knoblauch	H. M. Newhall & Co.	October 18, 1881	Oct. 18, 1881
1838	National Fire	New York	H. T. Drowne	P. J. Walton	W. J. Dutton	May 12, 1879	May 12, 1879
1871	National Fire	Hartford	M. Howard	J. Nichols	Meadwiley, Phelps & Co.	August 5, 1874	Aug. 5, 1874
1862	National Marine	London	H. W. Petre	Wm. Gray	Gutte & Frank	October 9, 1882	Oct. 9, 1882
1869	New Hampshire Fire	Manchester, N. H.	J. A. Weston	J. C. French	Chas. A. Laton	Nov. 3, 1886	Nov. 3, 1886
1878	New Zealand	Auckland	J. Williamson	G. P. Pierce	Hugh Craig	March 27, 1885	March 27, 1885
1850	Niagara Fire	New York	P. Notman	W. Pollock	Spencer & Herold	October 18, 1876	Oct. 18, 1876
1822	North American	Boston	A. Hooker	E. S. Partridge	K. K. Butler	March 27, 1884	March 27, 1884
1809	North British and Mercantile	London	G. H. Burnett	F. W. Lance	Thos. C. Grant	Sept. 28, 1868	Oct. 15, 1862
1863	North China	Shanghai	K. H. Layers	Alex. Hume	Macondray & Co.	June 15, 1876	June 15, 1876
1836	Northern	London	Sir Wm. Miller	J. Valentine	Robt. Dickson	Sept. 26, 1868	May 1, 1867
1868	North German Fire	Hamburg	T. Nordheim	C. Fryer	W. Speyer	Sept. 26, 1872	Sept. 26, 1872
1797	Norwich Union	Norwich, England	R. S. Patterson	C. R. Gilman	E. W. Carpenter	July 13, 1877	July 13, 1877
1877	On Tai	Hong Kong	Lee Sing	Ho Amei	Lai Hing Long & Co.	Nov. 22, 1877	Nov. 22, 1877

The Insurance Commission.

Year of Organization	Name.	Location.	President.	Secretary.	Agent for California.	Date of Certificate issued by Insurance Commissioner.	Commenced business in California.
1882	Oregon Fire and Marine	Portland	L. White	E. Hall	Hutchinson & Mann	August 25, 1883	Aug. 27, 1883
1863	Orient	Hartford	G. B. Whiting	G. H. Boswell	Geo. D. Dornin	March 10, 1882	March 10, 1882
1853	Pacific Fire	New York	T. F. Jeremiah	F. T. Stinson	Bella V. Wall	March 23, 1882	March 23, 1882
1825	Pennsylvania Fire	Philadelphia	J. Devereux	J. L. Thompson	Brown, Craig & Co.	Dec. 30, 1875	Dec. 30, 1875
1833	Phenix	Brooklyn	S. Crowell	P. Shaw	Brown, Craig & Co.	Nov. 9, 1868	Nov. 23, 1868
1854	Phenix	Hartford	H. Kellogg	D. W. C. Skilton	A. E. Magill	July 16, 1868	June 25, 1868
1782	Phenix	London	G. A. Fuller	W. C. McDonald	Butler & Haldan	Dec. 22, 1879	Dec. 22, 1879
1872	Prescott	Boston	F. H. Stevens	W. C. Harris	E. E. Potter	April 22, 1881	April 25, 1881
1799	Providence-Washington	Providence, R. I.	J. H. DeWolf	J. B. Branch	W. J. Dutton	Dec. 26, 1874	Dec. 31, 1874
1845	Prussian National	Stettin	G. Barch	O. Noeltner	Hirschfeld & Jacoby	Nov. 15, 1884	Nov. 15, 1884
1858	Queen	Liverpool	J. A. Moynahl, C. M.	Manager	Robt. Dickson	March 20, 1874	March 20, 1874
1863	Reliance Marine	Liverpool	L. H. Bailey	T. W. Dixon	Henry Lund	Dec. 19, 1881	Dec. 19, 1881
1845	Royal	Liverpool	J. H. McLaren	Digby Johnson	E. W. Carpenter	June 23, 1869	June 23, 1869
1865	Saint Paul	St. Paul, Minn.	C. H. Bigelow	C. B. Gilbert	Hutchinson & Mann	Sept. 23, 1872	Sept. 23, 1872
1829	Scottish Union and National	Edinburgh	J. M. McCandlish	J. K. Macdonald	Manheim, Staples & Co.	July 14, 1881	July 14, 1881
1875	Sea	Liverpool	R. P. Wood	W. Bates	Meyer, Wilson & Co.	July 19, 1876	July 24, 1876
1841	Security	New Haven	C. S. Leete	H. Mason	W. Macdonald	Jan. 12, 1877	Jan. 12, 1877
1872	South British Fire and Marine	Auckland	W. C. Daldy	G. Johnson	J. D. Macpherson	August 28, 1872	Aug. 28, 1872
1882	Southern	New Orleans	E. Miltenberger	S. Meticher	J. C. Jennings & Co.	Dec. 7, 1880	Dec. 7, 1880
1849	Springfield Fire and Marine	Springfield, Mass.	J. N. Dunham	S. J. Hall	Jacobs & Easton	April 6, 1881	April 6, 1881
1871	Standard Marine	Liverpool	W. Watson	J. Glen	J. D. Spreckels & Bros.	June 28, 1883	June 25, 1883
1882	Straits	Singapore	Jno. Anderson	W. Mactavish	Geo. Marcus & Co.	July 5, 1884	July 5, 1884
1866	Svea Fire and Life	Gothenburg, Swed.	C. O. Kjellberg	E. Berg	A. M. Philip	Sept. 22, 1882	Sept. 22, 1882
1710	Sun Fire Office	London	J. J. Guile, U. S. Manager		Hutchinson & Mann	Feb. 28, 1880	Feb. 28, 1880
1875	Sun Mutual	New Orleans	J. I. Day	D. Carpenter	Jno. C. Jennings & Co.	April 13, 1880	April 13, 1880
1863	Switzerland Marine	Zurich	R. Naef	H. Kaiser	H. W. Sye	October 2, 1871	[illegible]
1871	Teutonia	New Orleans	W. B. Schmidt	A. P. Kundl	Hutchinson & Mann	April 19, 1878	April 19, 1878
1860	Thames and Mersey	Liverpool	T. S. Rogerson	J. Kirkman	W. G. Harrison	August 21, 1872	Aug. 21, 1872
1836	The Marine	London	I. R. Englefield	H. J. Lodge	G. W. McNear	Sept. 14, 1872	Sept. 14, 1872
1865	Traders	Chicago	E. Buckingham	R. J. Smith	W. F. Hood	June 6, 1876	June 6, 1876
1872	Transatlantic Fire	Hamburg	W. Jacobsen	J. Wunderer	Geo. Marcus & Co.	August 2, 1872	Aug. 2, 1872
1872	Transatlantic Marine	Berlin	E. Bergenberg	J. A. Fischer	Thannhauser & Co.	June 21, 1873	June 21, 1873
1804	Union	Philadelphia	W. S. Hassall	J. M. Cowell	Jacobs & Easton	October 17, [illegible]	Oct. 17, [illegible]
1874	Union	Hong Kong	F. Sette	N. J. Ede	Page Brothers	Dec. 18, 1883	Dec. 18, 1883
1877	Union Fire and Marine	Christchurch, N. Z.	J. T. Peacock	W. G. Murray	L. L. Bromwell	Feb. 27, 1882	Feb. 27, 1882
1863	Union Marine	Liverpool	T. D. Hornby	W. Gow	E. L. Woods	July 3, 1873	July 3, 1873
1872	United Fire Reassurance	Manchester	T. Spinks	J. N. Lane	Hutchinson & Mann	July 29, 1881	July 29, 1881
1824	United States Fire	New York	W. W. Underhill	G. E. Cox	R. L. Beck & Sons	April 7, 1882	April 7, 1882
1861	Universal Marine	London	Sir J. Lubbock	A. Tower	W. H. Chapman	October 1, 1877	Oct. 1, 1877
1821	Washington Fire and Marine	Boston	J. Sawtell	A. W. Damon	Geo. D. Dornin	Nov. 1, 1877	Nov. 1, 1877
1837	Westchester Fire	New York	G. R. Crawford	J. Q. Underhill	A. C. Donnell & Co.	March 28, 1882	March 28, 1882
1851	Western	Toronto	A. M. Smith	J. Boomer	Butler & Haldan	Jan. 12, 1877	Jan. 12, 1877
1852	Williamsburgh City Fire	Brooklyn	E. Briggs	N. W. Messerole	R. F. Fowler	Feb. 1, 1882	Feb. 1, 1882
1862	Yangtsze	Shanghai	G. H. Wheeler	Russell & Co.	Macondray & Co.	October 23, 1882	Sept. 14, 1882
1868	Pacific Mutual Life	San Francisco	Geo. A. Moore	J. N. Patton		June 28, 1868	Feb. 3, 1868
1850	Ætna Life	Hartford	M. G. Bulkeley	J. L. English	Jas. H. Stevens	March 27, 1872	March 27, 1872
1864	Brooklyn Life	New York	W. M. Cole	W. Imelder	J. J. Bryant	Nov. 12, 1874	Nov. 12, 1874
1846	Connecticut Mutual Life	Hartford	J. L. Greene	W. G. Abbot	J. L. Foy	June 27, 1868	June 27, 1868
1859	Equitable Life	New York	H. B. Hyde	W. Alexander	Scotte & Flora	July 8, 1870	July 8, 1870
1860	Germania Life	New York	H. Wesendonck	C. Sherrone	J. Jacobs	Feb. 11, 1873	Feb. 11, 1873
1866	Hartford Life and Annuity	Hartford	F. B. Pierce	S. Hall	T. Whitworth	Nov. 17, 1883	Nov. 17, 1883
1850	Manhattan Life	New York	J. M. McLean	H. Y. Wemple	Jno. Landers	August 2, 1875	Aug. 2, 1875
1845	Mutual Benefit Life	Newark	Amzi Dodd	E. L. Dobbins	J. Maxwell, Jr.	Sept. 7, 1868	Sept. 7, 1868
1842	Mutual Life	New York	R. A. McCurdy	W. J. Easton	A. B. Forbes	July 1, 1868	July 1, 1868
1848	National Life	Montpelier, Vt.	Chas. Dewey	G. W. Reed	S. A. Mattison	June 11, 1880	June [illegible]
1835	New England Mutual Life	Boston	B. F. Stevens	J. M. Gibbens	D. E. Field	Sept. 26, 1867	June 17, 1867
1843	New York Life	New York	W. H. Beers	A. H. Welch	A. C. Hawes	August 24, 1875	Aug. 26, 1875
1857	Northwestern Mutual Life	Milwaukee	H. L. Palmer	J. W. Skinner	C. M. Smith	May 23, 1867	May 23, 1867
1863	Travelers	Hartford	J. G. Batterson	R. Dennis	W. W. Haskell	July 19, 1875	July 19, 1875
1867	Union Central Life	Cincinnati	John Davis	E. P. Marshall	C. H. Stewart	Feb. 2, [illegible]	Feb. 2, [illegible]
1848	Union Mutual Life	Portland, Me.	J. E. DeWitt	H. D. Smith	John Bowes	Sept. 16, 1868	Sept. 16, 1868
1850	United States Life	New York	G. H. Burford	C. P. Fraleigh	J. W. Howell	May 14, 1868	May 14, 1868
1860	Washington Life	New York	W. A. Brewer, Jr.	C. Munn	Jas. H. Gray	Feb. 5, 1882	Feb. 5, 1882
—	Phoenix Mutual Life	Hartford			E. P. Gray	August 28, 1880	Aug. 28, 1880
1885	Pacific Surety	San Francisco	W. Freund	E. F. Green		August 1, 1885	Aug. 1, 1885
1866	American Steam Boiler	New York	W. K. Lothrop	V. M. Schenck	Conrad & Mandell	October 12, 1884	Oct. 12, 1884
1884	American Surety	New York	R. A. Elmer	F. N. Nugent	H. F. Osborn	Dec. 5, 1885	Dec. 5, 1885
1876	Fidelity and Casualty	New York	W. M. Richards	J. M. Crane	J. R. Garnier	March 4, 1880	March 4, 1880
1866	Hartford Steam Boiler	Hartford	J. M. Allen	J. B. Pierce	Hutchinson & Mann	Nov. 8, 1882	Nov. 8, 1882
1871	Metropolitan Plate Glass	New York	H. Harteau	[illegible] H. Taylor	Hutchinson & Mann	May 6, 1879	May 6, 1879

The Pacific Insurance Union.

THE demoralization of the fire insurance business caused by the sharp competition of rival companies was such that the companies were at times unable to make any profits and the safety of the assured was imperilled. The "compact" system, as it is called, originated in the North Western States where it is applied to single cities or small districts. Its central idea is the criticism of all business transacted by all the members by a disinterested and competent manager, who also has the power of fixing rates for all alike, instead of leaving each member to be his own judge of the value of risks and of his own fidelity to the common obligations. It was long believed here that this idea could be so enlarged and elaborated as to regulate the entire business of this Coast, but at first it met with no encouragement, and it was found that if the plan was to succeed it must be gradually worked out. So, early in 1883, it was moved in the old Board of Underwriters that one of the standing committees be instructed to investigate the compact system at the East, and devise a plan for its adoption at the city of Portland, Oregon, where the business had long been demoralized and unprofitable. The committee wrote a few letters and received favorable answers, but finally reported that the agitation of the matter was premature, and asked to be excused from its further consideration. Later it was moved to appoint a special committee of seven with power to add to its number, and this committee should be required to perform this work. The motion was adopted and C. T. Hopkins was appointed chairman of the committee.

Six months of continual meetings followed. Several members of the committee dropping out in despair, others were called to their places. So many alterations were made to the first draft, that the printer's bill for a four-page report was over $200. Partial reports were made to the Board from time to time. At last the work was completed, adopted and signed, after infinite difficulty in procuring the signatures of two or three of the fifty companies doing business in Portland. Alfred Stillman was elected manager, and so well did the scheme work that every one was pleased with the results, and in less than a year the whole of Oregon and Washington Territory were placed under the management of Mr. Stillman. After a few months of satisfactory experience in this district, it was again moved in the Board that a special committee should be appointed to adopt the compact system to the whole of the Coast, and C. T. Hopkins was again appointed chairman of the committee. The agony of the previous year was repeated with an intensity proportioned to the greater interests involved, but by January 1885, complete success crowned the effort. All the one hundred and eight companies doing business on the Coast, representing over $350,000,000 of assets and having a revenue of $6,000,000 annually, finally enrolled themselves under the banner of the "Compact." Alfred Stillman was promoted to the office of General Manager, and since then the stability of the Fire Insurance business on the Pacific has been secured in a manner as yet unequalled in any of the other commercial centres of the world. Chas. R. Story, Secretary of the Home Mutual Insurance Company was the first President, and was succeeded by Captain Arthur Magill, Manager of the Home & Phenix Insurance Companies; the present incumbent, Charles D. Haven, resident Secretary of the Liverpool, London and Globe Insurance Company, was elected first Secretary and still holds that office.

The Board of Fire Underwriters.

OF SAN FRANCISCO.

THIS Board was organized January 11th, 1861, with the following officers: President, W. Lane Booker; Vice-President, C. A. Low; Secretary, W. H. Tillinghast; Treasurer, Morris Speyer.

The members of the Board were: Falkner, Bell & Co., W. B. Johnson, W. Lane Booker, Alsop & Co., Morris Speyer, C. A. Low & Co., E. H. Parker, B. F. Low, R. B. Swain & Co., John Fowler, B. R. Nisbit, J. R. Garniss, Bigelow & Bro., Wm. H. Tillinghast, R. H. McGill, S. B. Dell, E. W. Burr, Geo. C. Boardman, Jon. Hunt, A. J. Ralston, Wm. Holdredge, C. R. Bond.

The functions of the Board are two fold. First—To act as a supervisory board over all local insurance boards in any of the States and Territories of the Pacific Coast, and over all points in said States and Territories where no local boards exist. Second—To act as a local insurance board for the City and County of San Francisco.

Its objects are the establishment and maintenance of adequate and equitable rates for insurance, the promotion of harmony and correct practices among its members, and generally the improvement and elevation of the fire insurance business on the Pacific Coast. Through its committees on fire department, fire ordinances and water supply, on arson and on legislation, it has accomplished a great amount of good in promoting the effi-

The Board of Fire Underwriters.

OF SAN FRANCISCO.

ciency of fire departments; in causing the enacting and enforcement of proper fire ordinances; in examining and reporting on the adequacy of the water supply in cities and towns; in the establishment of fire patrols, at the sole cost of the underwriters, for the preservation of property, whether insured or not, from loss or damage by water at fires; in offering and paying rewards for the apprehension and conviction of incendiaries; in promoting wise insurance legislation by the State legislatures, and in preventing the passage of mischievous insurance laws. From 1877 to 1882, through the instrumentality of this Board, 74 incendiaries, who otherwise would probably have gone unwhipped of justice, have been convicted and sentenced. This Board has never sought the aid of the legislative authorities of cities and states from purely selfish motives, but its work in that direction has always been as much in the interest of the general public as for the protection of its own business. Since the organization of the Pacific Insurance Union, most of the work formerly done by the Board of Underwriters has fallen to the younger organization, though the Board of Underwriters still continues in active operation, elects the fire marshal, and transacts such other business as is not in the functions of the Pacific Insurance Union. The present president of the Board is D. J. Staples, President of the Fireman's Fund Insurance Company. C. D. Haven, resident secretary of the Liverpool, London and Globe Insurance Company is the secretary. Both gentlemen have occupied their respective positions for the past twelve years.

Fire Underwriters' Association

OF THE PACIFIC.

IN October, 1875, Virginia city, Nevada, was visited by a most disastrous conflagration, which called to the ruins some thirty odd adjusters representing the different companies doing business on the Coast. For the purpose of mutual protection and to facilitate the adjustment of the recent losses, the adjusters called a meeting on the 28th of October, 1875, in the palace car which was sidetracked and occupied by a number of them. B. F. Low was called to the chair and Col. J. W. Staples was chosen as Secretary. Daily meetings were had, and so great was the advantage derived from them that the Fire Underwriters Association of the Pacific became the natural outgrowth of the gathering.

On November 13th, 1875, a meeting was called looking to the permanent organization, and a committee consisting of L. L. Bromwell, H. H. Bigelow and J. R. Garniss was appointed to draft a constitution and by-laws, and February 23d, 1876, made their report which was adopted, and the Fire Underwriters' Association of the Pacific was permanently organized as a means "of disseminating valuable information, and elevating and promoting the interests of its members." The first officers elected were B. F. Low, President; H. H. Bigelow, Vice-President; J. W. Staples, Secretary.

Founded on the broadest principles of united effort, and having for its object the promotion of harmony and good practice in the profession, the interchange of views, opinions and personal experience, the discussion of topics of interest to the profession, the Fire Underwriters' Association has corrected abuses, induced thought, corrected practices, produced valuable essays and statistics, and from its very inception has steadily increased in members and influence.

The following is the list of the officers of the Association since its organization:

1876.

B. F. Low, President; H. H. Bigelow, Vice-President;
J. W. Staples, Secretary.

1877.

Geo. D. Dornin, President; W. L. Chalmers, Vice-President;
J. W. Staples, Secretary.

1878.

A. B. Flint, President; Ed Brown, Vice-President;
J. W. Staples, Secretary.

1879.

C. T. Hopkins, President; A. D. Smith, Vice-President;
J. W. Staples, Secretary.

1880.

G. W. Spencer, President; E. W. Carpenter, Vice-President;
J. W. Staples, Secretary.

1881.

L. L. Bromwell, President; Geo. F. Grant, Vice-President;
J. W. Staples, Secretary.

1882.

Geo. F. Grant, President; E. W. Carpenter, Vice-President;
J. W. Staples, Secretary.

Fire Underwriters' Association

OF THE PACIFIC.

1883.
E. W. CARPENTER, President; WM. SEXTON, Vice-President;
R. H. NAUNTON, Secretary.

1884.
WM. SEXTON, President; C. MASON KINNE, Vice-President;
C. P. FARNFIELD, Secretary.

1885.
C. MASON KINNE, President; E. P. CLARK, Vice-President;
R. H. NAUNTON, Secretary.

1886.
Z. P. CLARK, President; J. W. STAPLES, Vice-President;
R. H. NAUNTON, Secretary.

1887.
J. W. STAPLES, President; W. L. CHALMERS, Vice-President;
BERNARD FAYMONVILLE, Secretary.

Ancient History and Growth of Local Fire Insurance Companies.

UNDER the above caption the following article prepared for the "Knapsack" by Chas. D. Haven was read before the eleventh annual meeting of the Fire Underwriters' Association, held about a year ago:

Thirty years ago, on the 6th of January, 1857, all the agents engaged in the fire insurance business in San Francisco, met and formed the first fire insurance organization which was established in the Pacific Coast States, which they named "The Board of Fire Insurance." These agencies were only nine in number, and represented only twelve fire insurance companies, viz.: Continental, represented by C. Adolphe Low; Phenix, represented by E. W. Crowell; Home, Niagara, Washington and Park, represented by Jonathan Hunt; Liverpool and London, represented by Joshua P. Haven; Royal, represented by McKinley, Garriock & Co.; Imperial, represented by Falkner, Bell & Co.; Monarch, represented by William Lane Booker; Northern, represented by Smith Bros. & Co.; Unity, represented by Dickson, DeWolf & Co. Joshua P. Haven was the President of the association, and E. R. Falkner was its Secretary. Not one of these agents is now doing a fire insurance business here.

Some of the persons engaged in our profession in those days seem to have had methods for obtaining business similar to those said to be practiced by members of our fraternity at the present time; for, on the 24th of June of the same year in which they were organized, we find that they passed the following resolution, viz.:

Resolved—That the payment by a company or its agent of the stamp required upon a policy, without exacting the tax from the assured, will be regarded by this Board as a violation of its rules, being in fact a reduction of the rate of premium agreed upon between the members of the Board, and that a copy of this Resolution be served upon each member.

The wholesome rule of the Pacific Insurance Union, requiring a delinquent to pay a fine for an alleged deviation, and afterwards prove his innocence in order to recover the amount of the fine, was not one of the rules in force at that time.

The resolution calls to mind an old law of the State of California, imposing a stamp tax upon the policy of one dollar for each thousand dollars insured.

In the following year a local company made its appearance in our midst. The California claims to be the oldest local company, but it will have to yield this claim, for it is a fact, of which probably none of the underwriters of the present day are aware, that the first fire insurance company incorporated under the laws of the State of California was the German Mutual Fire Insurance Company of San Francisco, which was organized July 12th, 1858. As this was the first local company, I will give a few facts of its history. Its President was J. W. G. Schulte; Vice-President, Frederick Meyer; Secretary, John Kohlmoss; its Treasurer was our well known townsman, Nicholas Van Bergen; its office was at No. 136 Washington street.

This company was evidently an aristocratic corporation, as it took pains to inform the public by an advertisement in one of our early directories, that its office hours were from 2 o'clock to 3 o'clock P. M. only. How refreshing it would be to have such a regulation in vogue now-a-days. Just imagine this community now coming unsolicitated to your office to obtain the protection against fire, of which it is always in need, and which could only be obtained in one short hour out of the twenty-four! There would be no time for discussions about rates. What delightful serenity of mind those Teutonic underwriters must have enjoyed!

This company was not only aristocratic, but it was also exclusive. By the terms of its articles of incorporation, its business was confined entirely to the German population of this State. Whether it was that the moral hazard of our German residents of those days was so bad that they found it difficult to

Ancient History and Growth of Local Fire Insurance Companies.

obtain insurance, or whether they had so little confidence in the integrity of other nationalities as not to be willing to insure them, the records do not enlighten us.

We are frequently informed by the insurance press and by underwriters, of the great wisdom and skill of the Hartford underwriters; but let it be known that our German company distanced any Hartford company that ever existed in this, that they prosecuted a successful business and paid all their losses during a term of ten years without any capital whatever. They ceased issuing policies on the 25th of June, 1868, in consequence of being called upon by the first Insurance Commissioner of this State to have a paid up capital of one hundred thousand dollars, in compliance with the laws then recently enacted.

The incorporation of the California Mutual Marine Insurance Company (re-incorporated as the California Insurance Company in 1864) and the San Francisco Fire Insurance Company followed in 1861. The San Francisco left the insurance field quite too soon, after a remarkably conservative and profitable career. Its first Secretary and subsequent President, Mr. George C. Boardman is still an active and honored member of our fraternity.

Local companies now increased rapidly. The Merchants' Mutual, Fireman's Fund and Pacific were incorporated in 1863; the California Home and Home Mutual in 1864; the Occidental Union and National in 1865; the Builders' in 1866; the People's in 1867; the Mechanics' in 1868; the Oriental in 1869; the State Investment in 1871; the Commercial in 1872; the California Farmers' and Alameda County in 1874; the Western in 1878; the Oakland Home in 1880; the Sun in 1881; Southern California and Anglo-Nevada in 1885.

Only one of the local companies has been a disgrace to the profession, and that owed its paternity to that illustrious historian of Ireland, banker, underwriter and professed philanthropist, Thomas Mooney, Esquire. To the credit of the fraternity be it known that he never was recognized as an underwriter in good standing by his brethren in the business. The days of the years of his insurance career were few and evil; he brought discredit upon our profession but more upon himself

It will thus be seen that twenty-three fire and fire and marine insurance companies have been incorporated in the State of California — yes, twenty-four if we include the Merchants' Mutual, which took marine risks only. Of these twenty-four companies nine retired from business; three surrendered to the fire fiend at Chicago; one only was forced by the Insurance Commissioner to go into liquidation, and one never got out of its swaddling clothes; leaving ten now in existence.

Of the officers of the local companies who have gone "over the river," the older agents will remember Parker and Bond of the Fireman's Fund, Pierce of the National, Horner of the People's, Curtis of the State Investment, Stiles and Rothschild of the Occidental, Crowell of the California, Fay of the Union, and Scotchler and Bourne of the Merchants' Mutual.

Without intending to make any invidious distinctions in mentioning persons, it is certainly to the credit of local companies that they have given to our profession such honored names as those of Hopkins, Touchard, Boardman, Story, Scotchler, Parker, Fay, Staples, Laton and others. As a class the local companies have certainly shown an honorable record, which it is to be hoped will always be maintained. Most of them have been severely tried in the fire and not found wanting.

NOTE.—In the list of honored names none is brighter than that of Chas. B. Haven, to whom this Association is indebted for this bit of history.—*Editor Knapsack.*

Merchants' Mutual.

THE names of the defunct companies given in the above article, include the Merchants' Mutual Marine, whose honorable career needs more than passing attention. The company was presided over for years by Col. C. L. Taylor, now president of the Sun, and afterward by the late J. B. Scotchler, who at date of organization was made secretary of the company. It was incorporated April 20, 1863, with a capital of $500,000 in 100 shares, and the term of existence was fixed at twenty years. In July, 1867, the number of shares was changed from 100 of $5,000 each to 1,000 of $500 each. The first $250,000 of capital was paid in by stockholders and the other $250,000 from the earnings of the company, which were capitalized in 1867. The first dividend was paid in February, 1868, at the rate of 1 per cent., or $5 per share. These dividends were maintained uninterruptedly for forty-seven months. There were also four special dividends of $15 each. The first of these was paid in August, 1869, January and July, 1870, and January, 1871. The last regular dividend was paid in December, 1871. The dividends for the four years were as follows:

	Dividends.	Amount.
1868	11	$55,000
1869 (one extra)	13	65,000
1870 (two extra)	14	70,000
1871 (one extra)	13	65,000
Total (four extra)	51	$255,000

Following this period of prosperity came a period of adversity. The stoppage of dividends and other circumstances caused the stock to decline from 120 to 65. The company had agencies in New York, Liverpool, Hongkong, and one or two other foreign ports. The New York and Liverpool agencies were particularly unfortunate. The net loss on the New York and foreign agencies was $256,900. The company made all its profit in San Francisco, and if it had never gone outside of this city it would have been much better off. This unfortunate condition of things naturally made stockholders discouraged, and at the close of the year 1873, they voted that the company should wind up its affairs, and it immediately thereafter went into voluntary liquidation. The first division of capital was made in March, 1874, and the last dollar of the capital was paid to stockholders in January, 1875. Thus, within nine months the entire capital was returned to stockholders, as follows:

	Per Cent.	Amount.
March, 1874	25	$125,000
April	20	100,000
May	15	75,000
July	20	100,000
November	10	50,000
January, 1875	10	50,000
Total	100	$500,000

Had this been all, every stockholder would have been satisfied. But the company afterward paid three dividends from surplus saved after paying every liability, as follows:

	Per Cent.	Amount.
January, 1878	5.00	$25,000
March 31, 1879	2.00	10,000
February 9, 1881	.60	3,000
Total	7.60	$38,000

The company received its final discharge in Court in January, 1881, and the dividend paid in 1881 was the last act to be performed in the history of the incorporation. It would be gratifying to say as much of every incorporation which has passed out of existence in this city. Most of those that have retired, either voluntarily or involuntarily, have done so at the expense of stockholders. So far as learned there never was over $250,000 of the capital of the Merchants' Mutual Marine Insurance Company ever paid up. This money invested at 6 per cent. simple interest would have doubled during the interval. But invested as it was it did even better than that. For the $250,000 paid in during the year 1863, and subsequently, stockholders received as follows:

Regular dividends, 47	$235,000
Special dividends, 4	60,000
Capitalized earnings	250,000
Original capital	250,000
Surplus	
Total	$833,000

This is a pretty good show for $250,000. The original money paid in was not only returned but $583,000 in profit for the use of the same. Several other local insurance corporations have retired from business within the past twenty years, including the San Francisco, National Occidental, Pacific, Builders', People's, Oriental, California Farmers' Mutual and Western. The San Francisco and National paid off in full. The others are less cherished in the remembrance of stockholders. The Merchants' Mutual Marine did the best of them all, but it has now passed into history.

The Underwriters' Fire Patrol.

FIRE Patrols or Salvage Corps organizations have been in operation in the principal cities of the United States, such as New York, Boston, Philadelphia, Cincinnati, Chicago, St. Louis, for many years past. The same may be remarked with reference to Canada and Europe also.

The principal representatives of fire insurance companies in San Francisco, having considered the advisability of organizing such an enterprise in this city, concluded that it would be a wise move, so in the month of April, 1875, the Underwriters' Fire Patrol of San Francisco, began its operation. The first Board of Directors consisted of E. D. Farnsworth, D. J. Staples, A. J. Bryant, Wm. N. Olmsted, Chas. A. Laton, Tom C. Grant and Geo. T. Bohen.

This corporation has for its purpose, the discovery and prevention of fires, and saving property and human life from conflagration.

During all of the years which have transpired since 1875, the Fire Patrol has been under the supervision of a Board of Directors, seven in number, who are elected each year in January; the Board being selected from the principal representatives in this city of the several contributing insurance companies.

Captain Russell White has been in command of the force from the beginning, and his name and ability in this important enterprise, are familiar to all San Franciscans.

The Thirteenth Annual Report of the Fire Patrol for the year ending December 31, 1887, has just been issued, from which the following is quoted:

To the Members of the Underwriters' Fire Patrol of San Francisco:

GENTLEMEN: The Board of Directors take pleasure in handing to you herewith the Thirteenth Annual Report of the operations of this Corporation.

As remarked in last year's report, the year 1887 has also been one of considerable activity for the Patrol. Fires have been numerous and the losses somewhat severe. However, the Fire Patrol has succeeded in doing efficient work, and in accomplishing no small amount of salvage. In fact, under the efficient guidance and painstaking activity of Captain Russell White, the Fire Patrol has been enabled to make a handsome record; all of which should be, and doubtless is, most satisfactory to the contributors to this enterprise. We remark with satisfaction, that the apparatus, horses and other property belonging to this corporation are all in excellent order, as heretofore, ordinary wear and tear excepted.

Since our last annual meeting, the headquarters of the Patrol known as Station No. 1, has been changed from the southwest corner of Stevenson and Ecker Streets (where the Patrol has been domiciled during the past twelve years) to No. 106 and 108 north side of Jessie Street, between Second and New Montgomery Streets, where the Patrol now has elegant and commodious accommodations in the new two-story, metal-roofed, brick building recently erected, purposely for the Fire Patrol, by the trustees of the estate of William Sharon. The Directors are pleased to refer to Station No. 1 as being, without exception, the most complete and suitably arranged Fire Patrol building in the United States. This remark is made without any attempt at boasting whatever. It has been so acknowledged by all persons who have visited the building. Station No. 2 has also been removed from the north side of Grove Street, between Larkin and Polk Streets, to the northeast corner of Eddy and Polk Streets; the present location being more eligible than the former one. This enables the Fire Patrol to perform its duties in the section of the city alloted to Station No. 2 in a much more satisfactory manner. This change was alluded to in the last annual report. We are pleased to state that we have been enabled to pay for the steam salvage pump, also additional rubber covers (more than enough to make good those which were destroyed by fire during the year 1886), also the additional expense incurred by reason of the removals of Stations Nos. 1 and 2, without resorting to the levying of a special assessment, as was at one time believed would be necessary, and which was really provided for by the necessary authorization of this body.

As now arranged in every particular, the UNDERWRITERS' FIRE PATROL OF SAN FRANCISCO is in prime order to perform efficient service in every department of its work, and we are pleased to state that the members of the Patrol force are ever on the *qui vive*, and seem to be anxious to make the best possible record in every instance. In short, they perform their duties earnestly.

The Directors take great pleasure in remarking the continuance of good will and co-operation between the San Francisco Fire Department and the Underwriters' Fire Patrol of San Francisco. This remark has been made during so many years, in the Directors' report, that it really goes without saying. The same remark is also made with equal propriety as touching the Fire Alarm and Police Telegraph, Police Department, Fire Marshal, Telephone Companies, Board of Fire Commissioners and many others who seem to be interested in the success of the Fire Patrol. The Directors likewise desire to express thanks kindly and extend the sincerest congratulations to our old time friend, Chief Engineer David Scannell, Esq., also to all of his Assistants and subordinates in the Fire Department. Extending thanks likewise to Superintendent John Curran, Esq., and his Assistants of the Fire Alarm and Police Telegraph; also to Charles Towe, Esq., the efficient Fire Marshal, and to Chief of Police Crowley, and to the several officers and members of the Police Department, whose kindness and assistance have been noticed by the Fire Patrol many times in the past.

All of which is very respectfully submitted.

ROBERT DICKSON, *Vice-President.*
I. GUTTE,
E. E. POTTER,
E. B. HALDAN, } *Directors.*
A. C. DONNELL,
WM. J. LANDERS, *Sec. & Treas.*
CHAS. A. LATON, *President.*

The Directors elected at the annual meeting held January 19, 1888, are viz.: I. Gutte, A. C. Donnell, E. E. Potter, E. B. Haldan, Wm. J. Landers, Robt. Dickson, Chas. A. Laton. A re-election of last year's board.

One of the best features in connection with the successful management of this enterprise, lies in fact that there has never been the slightest jar or ill will between the San Francisco Fire Department and the Underwriters' Fire Patrol of San Francisco.

It is generally acknowledged that much of the efficiency of the Patrol system is due to the efforts of Chas. A. Laton, President of the Patrol, whose enthusiastic work in connection with several others in this direction, brought about the organization of the Patrol. His efforts were recognized by the members who elected him President of the Board of Directors at the first organization of the Patrol, a position he has constantly held since. W. J. Landers is the efficient Secretary.

Caspar T. Hopkins.

IN the opening chapters of this work are detailed the early career, and the valuable services Mr. Hopkins rendered in building up insurance business, while in the sketch of the California Insurance Company his connection with that corporation is briefly referred to. His efforts to found a local company were renewed after the failure of McLean & Fowler, which left a large demand, especially in marine insurance, for which there was no supply. Having conducted their marine business Mr. Hopkins felt that this want could only be satisfactorily supplied by local capital, and that if a good solid company could be got together here, it could do a splendid business. The difficulty was to overcome the reluctance of stockholders to face the terrible phantom of personal liability imposed by the State Constitution.

In fact Mr. Hopkins had already made several attempts to organize a local insurance company. In Sacramento he had proposed a scheme on the Lloyds plan, which, having been debated at two meetings of capitalists, was signed only by two men who were all that could muster the courage to venture on such perilous ground. One of these was Dr. R. H. McDonald now president of the Pacific Bank; the other was Charles H. Swift, afterward Mayor of Sacramento. His next attempt was in San Francisco while with McLean & Fowler. This plan involved the formation of a Trust Fund of $500,000, on the credit whereof he proposed that the firm should transact a marine and fire business, on a commission large enough to cover all expenses. But Fowler refused to concur in the scheme, and therefore no steps were taken to put it into execution. Immediately on leaving McLean & Fowler, he interviewed several capitalists with the plan of forming a Lloyds of a dozen men of undoubted wealth, for the purpose of taking marine risks only. This plan was favored by Nicholas Luning, James Donohue and Capt. Geo. C. Johnson, but at that time no additional names could be obtained. Those three gentlemen, however, found the required number of associates in the following year, and formed the California Lloyds with Gustave Touchard as secretary and attorney. Soon after the California Mutual Marine Insurance Company was formed, and Mr. Hopkins elected secretary. While this company was in process of incubation Mr. Hopkins accepted a contract from the Board of Fire Underwriters to prepare a fire map of seventy-two blocks of San Francisco, and deliver fifty copies thereof, lithographed, colored, mounted and bound, within six days. This was the first work of that kind done on the Pacific Coast. The plan was his own, being similar to the Sanborn maps of the present day, except that he used paper that was cross-ruled in squares, each square representing ten feet, instead of using a scale. Mr. Hopkins made all the surveys for this work himself and delivered it on time.

CASPAR T. HOPKINS.

Realizing Bacon's maxim that "every man is a debtor to his profession," and that underwriting could not be successfully carried on without a full and complete agreement between the several offices on all points of possible competition, Mr. Hopkins constantly labored in favor of boards, unions and compacts and uniform dealings with the public. He was the moving spirit in the formation of the Board of Marine Underwriters in 1864, of which he was elected secretary in 1865, and annually re-elected for twenty years. He wrote the original draft of the Constitution of the Board of Fire Underwriters, which was ridiculed for a time as the "Iron Clad Constitution," and had to be amended in many points to secure its adoption. He accepted the office of secretary of the Chamber of Commerce during 1868 and 1869, at a time when that society was badly demoralized. He suggested and worked out its reorganization on its present basis, and then secured its co-operation with the marine underwriters in fixing the rules and customs of marine insurance for the settlement of losses (which were originally drafted by him) in reducing the former exorbitant rates of commission in general average, and in the vigorous correspondence he inaugurated in the names of both bodies with the Light House department, which had for many years discontinued work on this Coast. The results of this last movement were the immediate erection of the lights on Point Reyes and Pigeon Point, and the subsequent continuance of the building of light houses and fog signals all along the Coast. He strongly advocated the revision of the State laws on Insurance, and in 1866 drafted the bill for the creation of the office of Insurance Commissioner, which became law. He wrote a pamphlet in 1867 directed against the formation of insurance companies merely for speculative purposes which had a marked effect. He formulated the tariff of the Board of Marine Underwriters and drafted the forms of marine policies that were used by all companies for many years. He wrote several pamphlets and many articles for newspapers, showing the advantages of Puget Sound for ship building, and caused the compilation of the "Specifications for building Vessels of Pacific Coast Timber" by the marine surveyors of San Francisco, the object whereof was to secure uniformity in building with a view to obtaining first-class ratings for our vessels. He collated, classified and published annually for eighteen years statistics of all the marine losses in which San Francisco was concerned, comparing the average loss on each voyage, inward and outward, with the current rates of premium. This and the "Specifications" were printed at the cost of the Board. He served for twenty years on the "Committee on Adjustments" of the Marine Board, whose examination and certificates gave currency everywhere to statements of general average made up at San Francisco. As president of the Fire Underwriters Association of the Pacific, which was organized by the adjusters and young men in 1875 merely as a social institution, he suggested that it be made a debating society for the discussion of the principles of underwriting. The idea was at once adopted, and for several years the annual two days' reading of studied essays on professional topics by the members, has done more to develop latent talent, and create a high intellectual ideal among the unusually able body of underwriters in San Francisco than all other influences combined. He instigated and partly conducted several heavy suits against the Pacific Mail Steamship Company. In one of these, the Costa Rica case, he recovered $42,000 for the losses caused to underwriters through reckless navigation, and in four others succeeded in breaking up the previous practice of that company, in charging fancy prices under the name of "salvage," whenever a towage service was rendered by one of their vessels to another in distress. He watched carefully over the pilot service, and, acting under the instructions of the Boards, succeeded in breaking one or two pilots for carelessness or intoxication, resulting in disaster to vessels under their care. He promoted the formation of the Merchants' and Ship Owners Steam Tug Company, which broke the back of a monopoly in towage. As chairman of a Committee of the Board of Trade and the Ship Owners, he did yeoman work in attempting to reduce the rates of pilotage at San Francisco, but always in vain. He wrote the pamphlet entitled "Suggestions to Masters of Vessels in Distress" which met with such general approval as to be reprinted by the Australian Underwriters, and by Lloyds Committee in London. He frequently lectured to the students of the Nautical school on marine insurance law, and on various topics to the young men in the University of California and the pupils of the High Schools of San Francisco and Oakland. As chairman of a Committee of the Board of Trade, Chamber of Commerce and Manufacturers Association, he prepared two elaborate reports on the causes of the decay of American shipping, and suggested the national legislation required to restore it. At the request of the Congressional delegation, Senators Miller and Farley and Representatives Page and Rosencrans, he put his recommendations in the form of a series of bills, which were introduced in both houses, and part of which were enacted in what is known as the "Dingley" law. His principal suggestions that only a national bounty or national postal subsidies to American vessels can restore the equilibrium disturbed at the expense of shipping by the tariff, that steamers so subsidized should be made capable of service as war vessels, and the price at which the government might appropriate them should be fixed at the time of the making the original contract for carrying the mails, and that all vessels carrying American apprentices should be released from tonnage tax according to a fixed scale, are now being agitated among shipping circles East, and will doubtless, sooner or later, find expression in legislation. He was also active in promoting the compact system, detailed in the sketch of the Pacific Insurance Union.

Notwithstanding the absorbing labor of his efforts for the good of the Insurance business, Mr. Hopkins found time for numerous self-imposed tasks in the broader field of the general good. He wrote in 1871 a work entitled "A Manual of American Ideas," intended to teach in popular form the principles of the American government and the duties of a citizen. This work has had a respectable circulation. A large and influential national society, called the "American Institute of Civics," has since been formed for the very purpose for which that book was written, of which its author is a counselor.

He was the promoter and president for two years of the California Immigrant Union, in 1870 and 1871, which raised and expended some $20,000 in advertising California to the immigrating classes in the East and Europe. This Association

Caspar T. Hopkins.

was one of the precursors of the efficient Immigration Society, conducted under the auspices of the Board of Trade. One of the causes of its suspension was the widely advertised opinion of its President, that Chinese immigration must be stopped, and the country filled only with white population, an idea then in advance of public opinion. He was the promoter and President of the Pacific Social Science Association, which in 1879–80 held fortnightly meetings for the reading of papers and discussion of topics bearing on the prosperity of California. This society had at one time about fifty members. It produced many good papers, some of which appeared in local magazines. One of these entitled "Taxation in California," by Mr. Hopkins, attracted no little attention at the time. It was a severe criticism of the principles of taxation embodied in the new State Constitution, with suggestion of an entirely different system. A separate publication, "An Alphabet of Principles of Municipal Government," intended to influence future freeholders' conventions in favor of a strong executive and limitations of the power of politicians in San Francisco, was the work of a committee of that Association, though principally written by its President. Its ideas have been worked out more or less in all three of the charters since prepared, and voted down by the people. The politicians have hitherto shown themselves too strong to be slaughtered by the adoption of any reformation in the city charter.

Mr. Hopkins was a prominent member of the famous "Committee of 100," which, during the summer of 1872 undertook to curb the power of the railroad, and was one of the committee of three (John S. Hager and R. G. Sneath being the others), that was sent on to investigate the affairs of the Atlantic & Pacific Railroad Co. with a view to its completion in the interests of San Francisco. Mr. Hopkins wrote the report of that committee which created great popular excitement at the time and resulted in the incorporation of the California Atlantic & Pacific Railroad Co., to whose stock several millions were subscribed. But the City Council refusing to allow a popular vote to be taken on the question of the city's interest in the scheme, it fell through, and for many years thereafter the Central Pacific was left undisturbed in its control of the railroad transportation of the Coast.

As chairman of a committee of the Chamber of Commerce, in 1873 he conducted an investigation and prepared an elaborate report on "Fares and Freights," with bills for Legislative action, creating a Board of Railroad Commissioners. This report had the immediate effect of preventing the passage of the "Freeman bill" fixing equal rates per ton per mile for all articles. In the following session Governor Irwin appropriated that report in his message to the Legislature and the bills passed in badly mutilated form—so changed in fact that the Commissioners appointed under it could do nothing for want of power. On their asking the next session for further power they were legislated out of office, and in due course the Constitutional Convention retaliated by creating a board with so much power, that the office has failed to be useful to the people. Mr. Hopkins found time to prepare several philosophical articles for local periodicals, to which, as a writer of studied papers on serious subjects, he was a valued contributor. Among the best of these were his articles on "Intellect vs. Influence," "Evil as a Factor in Evolution," and "Thoughts Toward Revising the Federal Constitution."

The above list of Mr. Hopkins' labors for the public good is far from complete. In early life he made his choice between popularity and usefulness. While his disposition was to be useful without the admixture of any selfish motive, other than the desire to be respected by thoughtful men, he has never been popular—in fact, he has always met with more opposition and criticism than with encouragement. He was never elected or even nominated to any political office, and even in his own profession was more the object of fear and dislike than of approbation or kind feeling. He knew how to say "No," and was remarkably deficient in tact. He was called by some a pessimist, but unlike that merely growling class of thinkers, he never pointed out an evil except for the sake of abating it. This suggestiveness is his leading characteristic. He has often been content merely to launch an idea, sometimes anonymously, or through another, very often through committees, and then let it take its chances of the actions of other men. In this way success has often been won by his ideas under such conditions as to cause the entire credit to be awarded to others. He naturally took the laboring oar in the numerous associations, corporations and committees in which he was continually working, and was generally the doer of the heavy work and the writer of the reports and resolutions. But he never received any acknowledgment or testimonial during his whole life until his retirement from business and from San Francisco, July 31, 1885. On that occasion his services were most handsomely owned by both branches of the Insurance profession at a complimentary luncheon, in beautifully enrolled addresses, and by the presentation of an elegant and costly service of plate. His portrait was placed in the rooms of the Insurance Union, and warm and effusive speeches were made by eminent gentlemen, both in and out of the profession. He was then sixty years old, worn out with hard work and suffering with a complication of diseases. He retired to his farm in Pasadena, Los Angeles County in Southern California, where he now resides, restored to health and in independent circumstances.

CONNECTICUT, LONDON, NORTHERN AND QUEEN INSURANCE CO'S
BANKERS AND
MERCHANTS
MUTUAL LIFE

FUND INSURANCE COMPANY

Fireman's Fund Insurance Company.

IT is eminently proper that a description of Pacific Coast Underwriting and Underwriters should commence with the Fireman's Fund, that institution being recognized by the business community, and freely acknowledged by its fellow underwriters as, perhaps more than any other, the representative Pacific Coast Company, its experience traversing the whole history of local fire underwriting upon this Coast, and including all the ups and downs of the business, and for nearly the entire term under the same leadership which still guides its progress.

When this company was organized, a quarter of a century ago, local fire underwriting was looked upon as a very hazardous experiment. At that time three marine organizations, the California Lloyds, the California Mutual Marine and the Merchant's Mutual Marine Insurance Companies, were experimenting quite successfully with marine insurance, and one small local fire insurance company, the San Francisco, was doing a limited business, writing no risk, however, outside the city limits.

DAVID J. STAPLES.

In 1862, Wm. Holdredge broached the subject to several merchants, of organizing a fire insurance company to be called the "Fireman's Fund." The idea was favorably regarded, and on August 15th, 1862, the incorporation papers were duly completed and filed. There appears, however, to have been some hitch in perfecting the organization, or some hesitation about launching out into business, for on May 3d, 1863, the papers were again prepared and filed, by the following incorporators: Henry Dutton, Daniel N. Breed, A. Himmelmann, R. H. Waller, Joseph H. Moore, James H. Cutter, Michael Lynch and William Holdredge, names well known to the older residents of San Francisco, but all of whose possessors excepting one (Mr. Moore) are now passed over to the silent majority.

The incorporators evidently thought that "in a multitude of councilors there is safety," for the $200,000 of capital was placed in charge of a board of fifty directors. In scanning the list we find the names of many who are still prominent in our community, among them John Barton (who has ever since retained, and still holds his position as a director and member of the Executive Committee), Samuel Brannan, E. Detrick, Henry L. Dodge, Arthur M. Ebbets, James C. Flood, B. M. Hartshorne, A. C. Nichols, Wm. Norris, James Phelan, Lewis P. Sage, Capt. John Short, J. M. Shotwell, Chief David Scannell, and Insurance Commissioner J. C. L. Wadsworth. The documents were filed with our late Governor, Washington Bartlett, then County Clerk. Wm. Holdredge was elected President and Chas. R. Bond, the then retiring City and County Assessor, was chosen as Secretary.

Most pioneer organizations are formed with the idea of operating upon some patent plan, afterwards found to be more or less impracticable (generally more), and the Fireman's Fund was no exception to this rule, the original idea, and which doubtless suggested the name, being to donate a portion of the net earnings from each city to the charitable fund of the volunteer fire department of that city, and then by prominently displaying a tin plate bearing the legend "Insured in the Fireman's Fund" upon each house taken under its protecting ægis, to secure the undivided efforts of the fire boys toward the saving of their property, to the confusion of those not so fortunate as to possess one of these fire proof policies.

May 3d, 1864, Samuel H. Parker, a prominent and very popular citizen, was elected president, and the charitable fund donation scheme being found wholly impracticable, was abandoned and on April 24th, 1865, the capital was increased from $200,000 to $500,000.

By the sudden death of Mr. Parker, in 1866, the company was left without a president, and on May 3d, of that year, David J. Staples was chosen vice-president and manager, W. B. Bourn filling the chair as temporary president. In 1867 Mr. Staples was elected president, a position which he has ever since held with constantly increasing credit and popularity to himself and the company.

In May, 1867, it was decided to establish a marine department, the business of the company having theretofore been confined to fire underwriting. Wm. J. Dutton, the company's present secretary, was engaged to take charge of this department which, from the start, has been uniformly profitable, and has contributed largely to the company's present prosperous condition.

In 1868, the company, which had up to that time confined its operations to the Pacific Coast, concluded to undertake a general business throughout the United States.

It selected as fire managers Messrs. Skeels, Bowers and Boughton, who planted an extensive agency system which reported to them at New York.

In conjunction with the Union and Occidental Insurance Companies its marine interests were confided to Lawson & Walker, the three companies issuing a joint policy under the name of the California Insurance Union. Messrs. Lawson & Walker had headquarters at New York, with agencies all along the Atlantic Coast from Maine to Texas, and in Canada and Great Britain.

On October 9th, 1871, the Fireman's Fund received its baptism of fire. Chicago was reduced to ashes, and with it perished many a company. Every Chicago local was melted out of existence. Many companies from abroad shared the same fate. Of the five California companies represented there, three collapsed, a fourth paid its losses handsomely, dollar for dollar, but at once withdrew all its eastern agencies, and restricted its business to the Pacific Coast. The Fireman's Fund alone, recognizing this gigantic disaster as one of the natural, though severe incidents to their business, at once prepared to meet their obligations as soon as adjusted. The company's capital was then $500,000, and its total assets were about $800,000. President Staples and General Agent Geo. D. Dornin were at once dispatched to Chicago, to ascertain the extent of the loss, and they soon learned, and telegraphed home that it would exceed half a million dollars.

An assessment of fifty per cent. was immediately levied, and they at once applied themselves to the adjustment of the losses, which were found, upon settlement, to aggregate $529,365. Within sixty days every loss was settled, and President Staples returned home, bringing with him a document signed by every Chicago claimant, complimenting the company upon the prompt and satisfactory settlement of their losses.

Meanwhile, the company having shown by this crucial test that its policies were, like the product and currency of its home, "pure gold," had advanced rapidly in favor throughout the East, where it bore alone the banner of Pacific Coast Underwriting, its policies being eagerly sought and its business rapidly increasing. It seemed fully launched on the high road to prosperity, when in November, 1872, and before its Chicago wounds were half healed, the great Boston fire called upon it for nearly $200,000. This was promptly met, and for nearly ten years thereafter the Fireman's Fund remained the only Pacific Coast company having agencies east of the Rocky Mountains. Within the past few years other California companies acting upon the well settled principle that the greater the distribution of risks the more safe the average, have one by one placed eastern agencies until now nearly all the Pacific Coast companies are writing eastern business.

WILLIAM J. DUTTON.

The California Insurance Union being dissolved by the failure of the Occidental Insurance Company through the Chicago fire, and the Eastern marine business not having proven profitable, it was then discontinued, and the company has since confined its marine business to its home office department, which has been uniformly profitable.

The largest Pacific Coast fire which has called upon the Fireman's Fund to give practical evidence of its merits, was the burning of Virginia City, October 26, 1875, when it paid the sum of $163,984, and the only annoyance which the company's stockholders experienced as the result of this rather heavy draft upon the surplus was the omission of one quarterly dividend. Since that time the company has never skipped a dividend, nor failed to show a healthy increase in both assets and net surplus at the end of each succeeding year.

The company's career has been a checkered one, its earlier history illustrating, and the latter avoiding the dangers to which inexperienced underwriting institutions are subject. Organized in 1863 with a capital of $200,000, this was increased in 1865 to $500,000. In 1871 the Chicago fire called for an assessment of $250,000, and in 1873, after the Boston fire, the capital was reduced to $300,000. In 1880 this capital, proving inadequate to its large business, it was increased to $750,000, and in 1886 the capital was again increased to a round million, where it now stands. The privilege of subscribing for this last increase at $30 premium per share, was distributed *pro rata* among the company's stockholders, and such as did not care to take their share found ready purchasers of their options at a still greater premium.

The year just past shows the largest business ever done by the company, its total net premiums having, for the first time, passed the "million dollar" line, and the Fireman's Fund enters 1888, with capital $1,000,000, and total assets $2,181,916.18, including a re-insurance reserve of $639,374.22, and a net surplus of $406,071.12, ranking among the first American companies in size, and with nearly, if not quite, the largest surplus and the largest income of any company organized west of New York.

As an evidence of the high regard in which this company is held at the eastern financial centres we cite the fact that more than one-third of its stock is held by eastern investors, and of this more than $150,000 is held in or about the city of Hartford, Conn., the acknowledged centre of American underwriting enterprise.

The Fireman's Fund deserves all the good will and support which it so handsomely receives from its large corps of loyal agents and patrons, and the Pacific Coast may well feel proud of a company showing such a record in the face of the disasters which have so continuously beset even our best underwriting institutions.

David J. Staples, President of the Fireman's Fund Insurance Company, is a native of Massachusetts, having been born in Medway, in that State, May 3d, 1824. As with the majority of the New England youth of that period he had his own fortune to carve. Before he had reached the age of eleven years both of his parents died, leaving David and his two sisters orphans. Feeling loath to live by the kindness of relatives, the boy, at the tender age of eleven, secured work in a cotton factory, and besides earning his own living assisted his little sisters. After two years of hard work in the factory he packed his bundle and started out to better his fortune, and, if possible, obtain an education. After an all-day walk he secured work from a farmer, his compensation being his board and clothes, schooling three months in the winter, and a new suit of clothes at the end of three years service. At the close of his term of service on the farm he apprenticed himself to a Mr. John Leach, of North Bridgewater, a shoemaker, and became an excellent workman, but finding that the labor was too confining, he, at the age of eighteen, apprenticed himself to William Mason, of Taunton, Mass., to learn the trade of a machinist. Having served his time with that gentleman he subsequently worked at his trade in Newton, Boston, Springfield and Salem, until 1849, when the gold find in California started him to this Coast. While pursuing his labors he found time to attend evening school, and added materially to his store of knowledge. His first business venture in this State was freighting to the mines in the South, from Stockton, with pack mules. In the spring of 1850 he purchased a Spanish grant on the Mokelumne river which he at once improved, and soon started east for his family, which consisted of his wife and an infant daughter he had never seen, and with them he returned to California in January, 1861. On May 3d, 1866, he was elected Vice-President and Manager of the Fireman's Fund Insurance Company, and a year later was made its president and since that date has ably presided over the destinies of that company, and his ability in financiering, and courage shown particularly during the trying times of the Chicago and Boston fires have been of the greatest benefit to his company. As President of the Board of Fire Underwriters, to which position he had been successively elected for the past twelve years, and still holds, his executive ability has been also clearly shown.

Mr. Staples, while in no sense a politician, has ever shown himself a public-spirited citizen, and everything looking to the public good finds in him a ready and earnest worker. He has, despite his objection to public life, occupied the position of Justice of the Peace of San Joaquin county, Vice-President of the State Agricultural Society, Port Warden of San Francisco, and Vice-President of the Society of California Pioneers, for which last named organization he has perhaps done more than any man in the State, except the late James Lick, whose friend and confidant he was for many years, and whose munificent bequests to the society were largely due to the influence of Mr. Staples. He is also a popular member of the G. A. R. The physical condition of Mr. Staples is remarkably good. He is now in the middle of life, and it may reasonably be expected that he has before him many years more of activity and usefulness. Mr. Staples is not lacking in the financial fruits of his extended business career, and is rich in the friendships earned by a long, honorable and useful life.

William J. Dutton was born at Bangor, Me., January 23, 1847. His father started for California in 1849, and in 1855 sent for his wife and family, including the subject of this sketch.

Mr. Dutton grew up in San Francisco, first taking our public school course, after which he attended the City College, then a flourishing educational institution, presided over by the Rev. Dr. Burrowes, where he took a college course in the classics and higher mathematics.

His father, Henry Dutton, who many of our readers will well remember as one of our prominent and highly esteemed citizens, was one of the original incorporators of the Fireman's Fund Insurance Company, and served for many years as its vice-president, and it is, therefore, not surprising that, when his son cast about for a business opening, he should gravitate toward underwriting.

He first obtained a position, at the foot of the ladder, in the office of the agency of the North British and Mercantile Insurance Company, of which the late Wm. H. Tillinghast was General Agent, and C. C. Harvey Manager. He remained there until May, 1867, when the Fireman's Fund Insurance Company having decided to establish a marine department, he was chosen as marine clerk.

At that time there were four other locals doing a marine business, and two or three agencies, which, however, were not actively pushed and did only a nominal business. The locals did practically all the business, of which the principal portion was by steam and sail from New York, the nearest approach to an overland railroad then being the Pony Express. The marine department was a success, and a source of profit from the start, and has continued so ever since.

In 1869, Mr. Dutton was elected Marine Secretary, and so remained until 1873, when, for convenience sake, his title was changed to Assistant Secretary, he, however, retaining special charge of the marine department. In 1876, Mr. Dutton was placed upon the Committee of Adjustments of the Board of Marine Underwriters, and has served continuously on the same ever since. In June, 1880, upon the retirement of the former secretary, to accept the management of an English agency, Mr. Dutton was elected General Secretary of the company, which position he still holds.

As a thoroughly posted and reliable underwriter, Mr. Dutton stands in the front rank of the profession, his uniform courtesy and urbanity making him extremely popular both in and out of insurance circles.

Bernard Faymonville, Assistant Secretary of the Fireman's Fund Insurance Company, was born in the State of Illinois, and his early education was obtained in that State. His His first knowledge of the insurance business was secured in the office of a real estate and insurance broker in the city of Chicago, where he placed risks in addition to his other duties. In 1877 he came to California and settled in the town of Fresno, in Fresno county. Shortly after his locating there he secured the local agency of fifty insurance companies, and after hard work and strict attention to business, he succeeded in building up one of the largest local agencies in the State. In 1884 the Fireman's Fund Insurance

BERNARD FAYMONVILLE.

Company recognizing his ability as an underwriter tendered him the position of special agent and adjuster, which he accepted and retained until the early part of 1887, when he was appointed Resident Special Agent of the same company, and assigned to the duties of the retiring Assistant Secretary. In July of the same year he was elected to the office of Assistant Secretary, which position he has since filled with credit to himself and to the entire satisfaction of the stockholders and directors of the company. In insurance circles Mr. Faymonville is very popular, and occupies the position of Secretary of the Fire Underwriters Association of the Pacific. As an underwriter he is careful and painstaking, and his future in the profession is assured.

NATHANIEL T. JAMES.

Nathaniel T. James, the Marine Secretary of the Fireman's Fund Insurance Company, was born in St. Louis, Missouri, but came to California when ten years of age. In January, 1866, he obtained a position in the California Insurance Company which then occupied their old office which stood on the same lot as stands their handsome building of today.

At that time the California Insurance Company was engaged in marine underwriting alone, and although the staff was small, the volume of their business was the largest on the Coast, and most excellent opportunity was offered for learning, under the leadership of C. T. Hopkins and Zenos Crowell, the correct rudiments of underwriting, which has since stood him in such good stead. In 1868, while still with the California he was appointed by Andrew Johnson, then President of the United States, a midshipman in the United States Navy, and was ordered to Annapolis for instruction; after the usual course of four years, he graduated No. 5 in his class, and was ordered to duty on foreign squadrons, where he served until the death of his father; he then returned to his old home in St. Louis and soon after arrival resigned his commission and entered into business.

In 1878, he returned to California and again tried the life of a sailor, this time as officer on board of merchant steamers; while so engaged he was again offered and accepted a position in the California Insurance Company. The Company was then engaged in both fire and marine insurance, and Mr. James was appointed special agent and adjuster of fire losses, which position he retained until Mr. Dutton, of the Fireman's Fund Insurance Company was promoted to the office of secretary, when Mr. James was offered and accepted the charge of the Marine Department of the Fireman's Fund Insurance Company vacated by him. In 1885, Mr. James was elected Marine Secretary of the Company; since that date he has devoted his time almost entirely to the marine branch of the insurance business and the study of the Maritime and International Law and Naval Construction. He is a member of the United States Naval Institute, and was one of the originators of the Association of Marine Underwriters, of which body he was elected President on its inception and was on the first annual election unanimously re-elected to the same position. His naval education and his service at sea, both in the United States navy and on board of merchant vessels, has been of much service to him in his chosen profession, of which he is not only very fond but also proud, and his practical experience in fire insurance as well as marine has helped him greatly in the legal matters which occupy so prominent a part of the duties and requirements of an underwriter.

The California Insurance Company.

LATE in 1860, by energetic work on the part of C. T. Hopkins, Dr. Samuel Merritt and one or two others, the California Mutual Marine Insurance Company was organized, but the articles of incorporation were not filed until February 14th, 1861. The Company organized with Dr. Merritt as President, and Mr. Hopkins as Secretary, and under a peculiar system. The subscribed capital was $200,000 in twenty shares of $10,000 each. These shares were held by twenty men, who each paid $1,000 in cash and gave their demand notes for $9,000 more. No one was allowed to sell out except to a man approved by the Board of Directors. No one was allowed to own a share unless he was worth $100,000, and no one was allowed to own more than one share. Only marine business was to be transacted, and only such risks were written as were approved by the Insurance Committee, nor loss paid without order of the Board. These peculiar features were found to be extremely embarrassing, and in 1864 the Company was re-incorporated under the title of California Insurance Company, its capital was paid up in full, for which an assessment of $60,000 sufficed after capitalizing the earnings. The shares were reduced to $100 each, and fire insurance was added to the marine business. The names of the "original twenty," the pioneer insurance stockholders, are to be remembered. They were: Dr. Samuel Merritt, * A. J. Pope, * W. C. Talbot, Wm. Norris, * Michael Reese, * John G. Bray, * C. W. Hathaway, * J. J. Felt, * H. B. Tichenor, D. C. McRuer, James Findla, * Levi Stevens, Charles Main, S. C. Bigelow, John Van Bergen, * Geo. H. Howard, * H. F. Teschemacher, Jonas G. Clark, * Charles F. Lott, * Peder Sather.

Dr. Merritt was succeeded in the Presidency after eighteen months service by D. C. McRuer, who resigned on his election to Congress in 1865. Albert Miller followed Mr. McRuer, serving most efficiently for one year, when, his health failing, Mr. Hopkins was promoted to the Presidency, and Zenas Crowell was elected Secretary. In 1866 the capital was increased to $300,000, of which $50,000 was capitalized from the earnings, and the Company began the payment of quarterly dividends, which have never been interrupted since, except for eighteen months in 1868-9, owing to excessive losses at a marine agency in New York.

Mr. Hopkins continued in the office of President until July 31, 1885, when he permanently retired from the insurance field.

L. L. Bromwell who succeeded Mr. Hopkins as President of the Company, and who still occupies that position, was born in Cincinnati a little over forty-one years ago. His early education was acquired in that city, and at the age of twenty he became classification clerk in the Cincinnati branch office of the Phœnix Insurance Company of Hartford. After two years of service in this and other clerical positions, he was in 1868

L. L. BROMWELL.

appointed special agent and adjuster of the same company, and in 1870 was sent to this State, filling the same post for the Pacific Coast branch of the Phœnix & Home Insurance Companies of Hartford and New York. In 1878 he was tendered and accepted the post of general agent of the California of this city, and in 1879 was elected Vice-President of the Company. On the death of Mr. Zenas Crowell the Secretary, the office of Vice-President was combined with that of Secretary, and Mr. Bromwell was elected to the position, which he filled until 1885, when upon the retirement of Mr. Hopkins, he was chosen to preside over the affairs of the company. During his twenty odd years experience in the business, he has acted as local agent in Cincinnati, O., Memphis, Tenn., St. Louis, Mo., and San Francisco, being one of the few Presi-

The names marked * are of those who have passed away.

The California Insurance Company.

dents who have actually served in the field. He is a Director of the Liberty Insurance Company of New York, and Manager of the Pacific Coast department of the Union Fire and Marine Insurance Company of New Zealand.

W. H. C. Fowler, the present Secretary of the California, is a native of England, and from 1867 to 1870 was with the firm of Dumas & Wylie, underwriters at Lloyds, London. From 1870 to 1872 with A. S. C. Waugh at New Orleans, as adjuster of marine losses. He located in California in 1874, and the knowledge of the profession gained by his services in the old world and the new, enabled him to at once enter the service of the California Insurance Company and he steadily advanced through various clerkships, until 1882 when he was elected Marine Secretary, an office which he filled with marked ability. In 1885, upon the elevation of Mr. Bromwell to the presidency, the directors recognizing Mr. Fowler's ability as an underwriter, and devotion to the affairs of the Company, unanimously elected him Secretary, a position he has since retained. His management of the office has fully justified the confidence reposed in him by the Company.

The company, always successful, has had new energy imparted to it by the vigorous policy pursued by the present management, and has of late greatly extended its eastern business in the marine line, while keeping pace with the growth of business at home. Its assets now amount to over $1,100,000, and its agencies are to be found everywhere on the Coast, and at all the leading centers beyond the Rocky Mountains. Its surplus as regards policy holders is $805,090.97, and its paid up capital is $600,000.

W. H. C. FOWLER.

Home Mutual Insurance Company.

WHEN obtaining a policy of insurance upon his real estate or stock of merchandise it is the main desire of the insured to obtain a maximum security at a mimimum rate, and to accomplish this he is careful to look into the record of the company with whom he places his insurance. A company whose record offers superior inducements to the property owner, is the Home Mutual of this city. The Company was organized in 1864. The name would imply that it is worked on the "mutual" plan, but such is not the case. It is a stock company with a paid up capital of three hundred thousand dollars. Its cash assets amount to $800,000 and its *net surplus over all liabilities* foots up over a quarter of a million dollars. The Company has just paid its 144th monthly dividend, to its stockholders, of one dollar per share. Its dividends are declared from its *interest and rental income*, the net earnings from the insurance business proper going to swell the surplus fund. Another point that should be considered by those about to place insurance with this company, is that while the face value of the stock is $100 per share, it is worth in open market $167.50 per share, and hard to obtain at that figure, its book value being $185 per share. The report of the insurance commissioner shows that this reliable company receives premiums on business on the Pacific Coast equal to any company, foreign, Eastern, or local, doing business here.

The active management of this Company is in the hands of men of much business ability and experience as underwriters. The President of the Company, General J. F. Houghton, enjoys the reputation of being one of the ablest financiers on the Coast.

GENERAL J. F. HOUGHTON.

He is by profession a civil engineer, and came to California in 1850. In 1874 he retired from mercantile pursuits and became president of the Home Mutual.

Chas. R. Story, Secretary of the Home Mutual, arrived in California in September, 1849, in the bark *La Grange*. Shortly after his arrival he established the drug house of Charles R. Story & Co., later the firm became Story, Redington & Co., and after the withdrawal of Mr. Story became Redington & Co., by which name it is known as one of the mammoth commercial establishments of this Coast.

Mr. Story has been for eighteen years Secretary of the company and much of its success is due to his ability as an underwriter. Devotedly attached to the science of insurance his spare moments are given to the study of his calling and many of the most important changes in the conduct of the business on this Coast have emanated from him. He was three times elected President of the Pacific Insurance Union and was one of the principal factors in its organization. Among insurance men he is accounted a studious, painstaking, and consequently, a throughly posted underwriter.

The Company's home office is located on Sansome near California street, and agencies are established all over the country. Property owners will be consulting their interests by placing their risks with the Home Mutual Insurance Company.

Branches having agencies reporting thereto have for over fifteen years been established at Oakland, San Jose, Los Angeles,

C. R. STORY.

Cal., and Portland, Or., each branch being a sort of local insurance company—a peculiar feature of the Home Mutual Insurance Company.

Anglo-Nevada Assurance Corporation.

THIS home institution was duly incorporated and organized on the fourth day of November, 1885, with a paid up capital of $2,000,000, and the following well-known gentlemen as Directors: J. W. Mackay, J. L. Flood, J. B. Haggin, Louis Sloss, J. Greenebaum, W. Greer Harrison, E. L. Griffith, E. E. Eyre, W. F. Whittier, G. L. Brander and John Rosenfeld. Wm. Greer Harrison was elected President, J. L. Flood Vice-President and C. P. Farnfield Secretary. In March, 1886, Mr. Harrison retired from the company and was succeeded by G. L. Brander as President, and W. H. Dimond as Director.

C. P. FARNFIELD.

Later Mr. Flood retired, and was succeeded by J. F. Bigelow as Vice-President and Director. In October, 1887, G. L. Brander severed his connection with the company and the following gentlemen whose names are synonymous with financial ability were placed in charge of the company's affairs: President, Louis Sloss; Vice-President and Managing Director, C. P. Farnfield; Secretary, Z. P. Clark; Directors, J. W. Mackay, Louis Sloss, C. P. Farnfield, W. F. Whittier, J. B. Haggin, W. H. Dimond, J. Greenebaum, E. E. Eyre, C. S. Neal, E. L. Griffith, J. F. Bigelow.

The affairs of the corporation are ably managed, and its career has been an example of the great principle that permanent success lies rather in prudent and conservative management, with just dealing and prompt adjustment of all losses, than in taking ill-advised risks, and lack of true economy and care in carrying on business. The corporation transacts a general fire and marine business, and its agents are to be found in all the cities and towns of the United States.

In addition to its capital of $2,000,000, the Anglo-Nevada has a reserve for re-insurance amounting to $455,310.66, and is in a most satisfactory condition considering the age of the corporation. The amount of fire premiums received for the year 1887 was $886,645, the premiums in the marine department footed up $121,060.88 for the same period, while the interest on capital, &c., reached the sum of $123,312.99. The loss ratio during the year was a shade under 50 per cent. The Anglo-Nevada occupies a leading position among the companies of the country, and has secured the confidence and esteem of the business public by the liberal adjustments and conservative writings which have ever characterized its transactions.

Louis Sloss, the President of the company, is one of San Francisco's best-known capitalists and business men, being the President of the Alaska Commercial Company. Further comment is unnecessary.

C. P. Farnfield, Vice-President and Managing Director of the Company, was born in the County of Surrey, England, in 1841. At the early age of fifteen years he became a clerk in the office of a Russian merchant in the city of London, and was assigned to duty in the insurance department of the business, and here his first knowledge of underwriting was obtained. Later he became purser on mail steamships, and for a period of ten years traveled in that capacity, visiting almost every country in the world. In 1871 he came to San Francisco and soon after secured a clerkship in the office of the Union Insurance Company. By his untiring energy and faithfulness in the discharge of the duties assigned him, he rose rapidly, reaching, before his withdrawal from the Union, the position of General Agent. Upon the organization of the Anglo-Nevada Assurance Corporation, he was tendered and accepted the position of Secretary of that company, and for two years so acceptably did he fill that office, that in October, 1887, he was elevated to the position of Vice-President and Managing Director.

Z. P. Clark, the Secretary, was born in the State of Ohio, in 1842, and was educated at Lawrence University, Wisconsin.

Anglo-Nevada Assurance Corporation.

The late civil war having commenced before he entered upon a business career, the young man enlisted as a private in the First Wisconsin Infantry, and served his country for four years, retiring on account of disability caused by wounds at Chickamauga, Georgia. After his resignation from the army he located at Nashville, and became local agent of several insurance companies, and for seven years devoted himself to the profession of underwriting in that field. In 1870 he came to San Francisco and established on this Coast a branch of the Widows and Orphans Mutual Life Insurance Company, which he conducted until 1874, when the company determined to retire from this Coast.

Re-insuring its risks in another company, Mr. Clark wound up his business and became the general agent of the Lancashire, Springfield Fire and Marine, the Orient, and several other companies. In 1878 he became special agent and adjuster of Hutchinson & Mann's Agency, which post he retained until 1881, when he was appointed Agency Inspector of the Commercial Union Assurance Company of London. In October, 1887, the Directors of the Anglo-Nevada Assurance Corporation tendered Mr. Clark the Secretaryship of that company, which he accepted, and now fills with credit to himself and satisfaction to the stockholders of the corporation. Mr. Clark is Assistant Adjutant General on the staff of Major General Dimond, Commanding Division N. G. C.

The Anglo Nevada was one of the first American companies to establish a Southern Department under the rapid improvement now taking place in that section. The wisdom of this move shows much discernment on the part of the managers of the corporation.

Z. P. CLARK.

Union Insurance Company.

MESSRS. John Parrott, James Phelan, L. Maynard, J. B. Haggin, George C. Johnson, N. Luning, James Otis, James Donahue, W. E. Barron, and J. Mora Moss, of the city of San Francisco, in May, 1861, entered into an association, known as the California Lloyds, the purpose of which was to assume, in individual proportion, marine risks (including war risks) under the management of Gustave Touchard.

In April, 1865, the Union Insurance Company of San Francisco was organized with a capital stock of 750,000, Caleb T. Fay, as president, Charles D. Haven, secretary, and the following gentlemen as Directors :—

J. Mora Moss, James B. Haggin, Lafayette Maynard, Nicholas Luning, Joseph A. Donohoe, Lewis Cunningham, Moses Ellis, Thomas H. Selby, Moses Heller, Charles W. Brooks, James Otis, Caleb T. Fay, William Smith, Jacob Underhill, Jacob Scholle, Michael Castle, J. Y. Hallock, John Parrott, Benjamin Brewster, Nicholas Larco, Myles D. Sweeny, Peter H. Burnett, C. Temple Emmet, Jonathan G. Kittle, Patrick McAran, James C. Conroy, William E. Barron, Joseph Seller, John Sime, George C. Johnson, Charles L. Low, Gustave Touchard, James Phelan, B. F. Hastings, L. H. Allen, Wm. C. Talbot and Wm. H. Gawley.

The company immediately commenced the erection of the building, Nos. 416 and 418 California Street, which they still occupy; this was the first substantial improvement on that street.

The Lloyds and the Union were so closely allied in business that it was thought desirable to unite their interests under one management, and accordingly, in January, 1866, the Lloyds was consolidated with the latter company, Mr. Touchard being retained as marine director, which position he continued to fill until elected president, on the resignation of Mr. Fay, in the following year, and has continued to occupy that position up to the present time.

Under the able presidency of Mr. Touchard the Union has become known as a successful underwriter, and has proved itself one of the staunch corporations of the country; having not only kept pace with the development and prosperity of the Pacific Coast, but also gradually extended its area of usefulness until at the present time, its policies are to be found in nearly all of the principal cities and towns east of the Rocky Mountains, side by side with those of other millionaire companies belonging to the older States.

GUSTAVE TOUCHARD.

(From a crayon portrait in possession of the Pacific Insurance Union.)

It was involved in the great Chicago fire of 1871, to the extent of $547,000, and discharged every liability immediately and in full. It has agencies throughout the country, and therefore draws its revenues from many sources, doing business on

JAMES D. BAILEY.

the principle that a company is bound so to limit and scatter its risks, that in any and every event the policy holder will be protected, and his just claims be paid in full. It accordingly discards all reckless and gambling methods, and stands by old fashioned conservatism, fair dealing and the prompt payment of just obligations.

That the company has been a grand success is shown by the fact that in twenty-two years it has paid dividends to the amount of $2,235,000, or nearly three times its capital.

Jonathan G. Kittle, the present Vice-President, is the senior member of the importing house of Kittle & Co. He has been identified with the Union since its organization, having been one of the original Directors.

James D. Bailey, Secretary, is a native of Boston, Mass., and came to San Francisco a young man, in 1861, to engage in business. Choosing the profession of underwriting, he entered the office of McLean & Fowler, the prominent insurance agents of that time, and, upon the organization of the Union Insurance Company, in 1865, applied for and was appointed to a clerkship. By a conscientious and prompt attention to the interests of the Union, he has been advanced step by step, through the several grades of special agent, adjuster and general agent, to the position of Secretary. Mr. Bailey holds a leading position as a fire underwriter, and that he has the confidence of his company is demonstrated by his long service in its interests, and the respect of his associates in the insurance profession.

The following well-known gentlemen comprise the present Board of Directors: Benj. Brewster, M. J. O'Connor, R. S. Floyd, John Barton, Adam Grant, Daniel Meyer, A. E. Sabatie, J. S. Hager, E. L. Goldstein, I. Lawrence Pool, A. M. Rosenbaum, Jos. Brandenstein, Charles Baum, James Moffitt, Isaac L. Requa, John Nash, H. C. Parker, W. M. Hoag, Nicholas Luning, E. Ransom, D. E. Martin, A. W. Foster, M. D. Sweeny, Bartlett Doe, Gustave Touchard, William Campbell, J. G. Kittle, Geo. C. Hickox, J. H. Freeman, A. W. Scholle, H. Maubec, I. Steinhart, C. A. Houghton, Cyrus Walker, Alexander Stoddard, R. Dinsmore and J. Martenstein.

The management of its Eastern department, comprising the New England States, New York, New Jersey, Pennsylvania, Maryland and West Virginia, is in the hands of Messrs. Roosevelt & Broughton, No. 44 Pine Street, New York, and the management of its Western department, comprising Indiana, Illinois, Tennessee, Kentucky, Missouri, Michigan, Kansas, Iowa, Nebraska, Minnesota, Wisconsin and Dakota, is in the hands of Messrs. Thos. & W. A. Goodman, No. 142 La Salle Street, Chicago.

Commercial Insurance Company.

OF CALIFORNIA.

THE Commercial Insurance Company of California, principal office at No. 439 California Street, Safe Deposit Building, was organized over sixteen years ago. At that time, numbering in its list of stockholders and directors were some of the foremost and wealthiest of San Francisco's merchants and business men generally. The list of Directors at the present time is as follows: Charles Main, of the firm of Main & Winchester; Geo. L. Bradley, Capitalist; H. B. Underhill, Attorney at law; W. L. Elliott, California Safe Deposit and Trust Company; Chas. Bogan, of Bogan & Company, merchants; A. Bocqueraz, of the firm of Shea, Bocqueraz & Co.; Peter Dean, President Sierra Lumber Company, also President Merchants' Exchange Bank, (in liquidation); C. Turner, proprietor Bay City Soda Water Company; John H. Wise, of the firm of Christy & Wise, wool commission merchants; E. M. Root, of the firm of Root & Sanderson, merchants; John Barton, President Union Pacific Salt Company; D. H. Haskell, town site agent, C. P. R. R. Co., and Pacific Improvement Company; W. J. Bryan, Superintendent O and O Steamship Company; A. W. Jee, Secretary Union Pacific Salt Company; L. Cunningham, of Shea, Bocqueraz & Co.; A. Y. Trask, Marine Surveyor; James Simpson, M. D.; B. L. Schmitt, Capitalist; J. C. Coleman, of Coleman Bros., Capitalists; N. Ohlandt, of N. Ohlandt & Co., merchants and manufacturers; B. P. Oliver, Real Estate and Capitalist.

The business of this company has been conducted with a rare degree of prudence, from the beginning until the present time, constantly meriting the fullest confidence of the public generally, and has received a very flattering patronage. The Commercial

JOHN H. WISE.

Commercial Insurance Company.

OF CALIFORNIA.

Insurance Company of California has agencies in the cities, towns and villages all over the Pacific Coast, as also in some of

CHAS. A. LATON.

the larger and more prosperous cities east of the Rocky Mountains. At the present time, the assets of this Company, which are invested in the most careful manner possible, approximate a half million of dollars. From the organization of the Company to December 31st, 1887, nearly two million dollars have been disbursed in loss claims, to the entire satisfaction of all parties, who have favored this Company with their business. Much more might be stated in the matter of details, but this is sufficient, and fully covers the ground. It may not be out of place to remark, however, that the Commercial Insurance Company of California has also been one of the best dividend paying corporations in the State of California, as has been evidenced by the regular monthly dividend of one per cent. upon the capital stock, year in and year out. The President of this Company is John H. Wise, member of the well-known and highly respected wool commission house of Christy & Wise, also one of the Board of State Harbor Commissioners. Mr. Wise is a gentleman of much popularity in the city and county of San Francisco, as also in the State at large, and is favorably known all over the Pacific Slope. The Secretary of this Company, Chas. A. Laton, has given twenty-seven years of his business life to the onerous duties which belong to the insurance business, and is too well known and appreciated in insurance circles, to require any extended notice here. Mr. Laton is also the Pacific Coast General Agent for the following named sterling fire insurance companies: Fire Association of Philadelphia, one of the strongest and oldest insurance corporations in America, with assets of the very best class, aggregating over four million dollars; New Hampshire Fire Insurance Company of Manchester, N. H., with assets of the best class, aggregating over one million and a quarter dollars. Granite State Fire Insurance Company of Portsmouth, N. H., good assets of about four hundred thousand dollars.

Sun Insurance Company.

OF SAN FRANCISCO.

AMONG the younger candidates for popular favor is the Sun Insurance Company, fire and marine, of San Francisco, which was organized February, 1882, with $300,000 paid up capital and the following strong directory: C. L. Taylor, President; J. N. Knowles, Vice-President; I. Steinhart, R. D. Chandler, Gustave Niebaum, J. B. Stetson, J. J. McKinnon, Francis Blake, E. B. Pond, Alfred Barstow and C. L. Dingley; E. E. Potter was elected Secretary and Treasurer. The same officers have continued in office ever since, and the same directors with the exception of Mr. Niebaum who was succeeded by Geo. H. Collins and Francis Blake, whose recent death caused a vacancy which was filled by the election of James Moffitt. Since its organization the Sun has received premiums to the amount of $1,623,703, has paid $562,722.09 in losses, and $97,500 in dividends. Its surplus as regards policy holders now amounts to $597,114.86. The constitution of the company provides that before declaring dividends twenty-five per cent of the net earnings must be set aside as a permanent reserve fund. No other United States company has this provision, and under it the

COL. C. L. TAYLOR.

Sun has now a permanent reserve fund amounting to over $40,000. The undivided profits January 1st, 1888 were $61,688.76. Besides its extensive and profitable business on this coast the company has flourishing agencies throughout the country east of the Rocky Mountains.

Col. C. L. Taylor, the president of the company, is one of the pioneer citizens of the State, having arrived here from Maine early in 1850. His early life in the east was devoted to the sea, and although almost a boy when he arrived here, he had risen to the position of master of a vessel.

He took an active part in early politics, although refusing office, and was Chairman of the Republican Committee for the first four years after its organization. In 1858 he was pressed, however, to accept office and he was thereupon elected School Director. In 1863 he was elected to the Board of State Harbor Commissioners, and of this was made President. At the same time he was elected to the presidency of the Merchants' Mutual Marine Insurance Company, which, however, he resigned to visit Europe and the French Exposition. In 1873 he was again elected to the Board of Harbor Commissioners, and in 1879 to a Supervisorship of the city.

In 1882 he was chosen as President of the Sun Insurance Company, which position he now holds, and he has certainly advanced, not alone the interests of this company, but of insurance generally by his work. Since that time Col. Taylor was also President of the Real Estate Protective Association, started

E. E. POTTER.

to fight corrupt contracts against the city. He has held several other honorable positions, such as Vice-President, Marine Underwriters, Trustee Chamber of Commerce, etc., and was Treasurer of the Republican State Central Committee during some of the most active campaigns.

Sun Insurance Company.

OF SAN FRANCISCO.

E. E. Potter, Secretary of the Sun Insurance Company, has been known in the profession on this Coast for the past fifteen years, and, as above stated, was one of the organizers and has been the Secretary and Treasurer of the company ever since its formation. He is also Pacific Coast manager for the Boston Underwriters of Boston, Mass., Williamsburg City Fire Insurance Company of New York, the Franklin Fire Insurance Company of Philadelphia, and the Michigan Fire and Marine Insurance Company of Detroit. The fire premiums for the Pacific Coast of the above mentioned companies under Mr. Potter's management for fifteen years have amounted to $1,755,007 with losses amounting to $559,556, making a loss ratio of less than 32 per cent which speaks for itself. This showing takes in about $51,801 paid on losses incurred by the great Virginia City fire in October, 1875. Mr. Potter is one of the Directors of the Underwriters' Fire Patrol, is Director and Secretary of the San Francisco Art Association, and holds several other positions of trust and honor.

State Investment and Insurance Company.

OF SAN FRANCISCO.

THIS well known and reliable home institution was organized in December, 1871, the corporation including such prominent and responsible citizens as Hon. A. J. Bryant, C. H. Cushing, Tyler

A. J. BRYANT.

Curtis, Peter Donahue, John Rosenfeld, and C. D. O'Sullivan. The capital was $200,000 at the organization, and subsequently raised to $400,000. The first president of the company was Tyler Curtis, who was afterwards succeeded by the late Peter Donahue, and he in turn gave place to the present head of the company the Hon. A. J. Bryant, who had for some years occupied the post of vice-president.

No man in San Francisco occupies a higher place in the esteem of his fellow citizens than Mr. Bryant. His popularity has been evidenced by the many high positions he has been called upon to fill. His fellow citizens deemed him a fitting person for the mayoralty of this city, and elected him to that place, and so well did he meet their expectation, and so able and satisfactory was his administration of public affairs, that he was re-elected to the office by a handsome majority. In politics Mr. Bryant is a straight out Democrat of the old school, and a man whose voice is listened to with marked attention in the councils of that party. In business circles he is regarded as a reliable, energetic business man and a financier of merit.

Charles H. Cushing, the secretary of the company, has occupied the position he so ably fills since the organization of the company. As an underwriter he ranks among the foremost on this Coast, and his reputation as an accountant was fully established years ago. His ripe experience, coupled with tireless energy, has materially aided in placing the company upon its present basis. The business of the company extends over not only the State of California, but covers every State and Territory west of the Rocky Mountains. The annual statement just issued for the year ending December 31st, 1887, shows that the income of the Company for the year amounted to $289,704.92, while the total expenditures reached $265,441.61, which included salaries, running expenses, dividends, etc., making a net gain of $23,263.31. The capital of the Company is $450,000 and its assets $552,000.12.

Premiums Received from Organization of Company	$4,086,410 13
Losses Paid from Organization of Company	1,505,074 79
Dividends Paid (since March 31, 1873)	553,489 34

The Southern California Insurance Company.

OF LOS ANGELES, CAL.

WAS incorporated February, 1885, with a capital of $200,000.00 and commenced business in March of the same year, with the home office located on South Spring Street, Los Angeles City. The original Board of Directors and Officers were:

Hon. John G. Downey,	ex-Governor California,	Los Angeles.
Hon. E. F. Spence,	Pres. First National Bank, and Mayor of	Los Angeles.
Hon. John Lawshe,	Capitalist,	Colton, Cal.
Wm. H. Perry,	Perry Mill Co.,	Los Angeles.
John Bryson, Sr.	Capitalist,	Los Angeles.
Nelson Vanderlip,	Capitalist,	Santa Ana.
Hon. P. M. Green,	Pres. Pasadena Bank,	Pasadena.
Isaac Fellows, M. D.	Capitalist,	Los Angeles.
F. C. Howes,	Cashier Los Angeles National Bank,	Los Angeles.
L. W. Dennis,	Real Estate,	Los Angeles.
H. C. Sigler,	Capitalist,	Los Angeles.
H. C. Sigler, President.		Matthew Long, Secretary.
E. F. Spence, Vice-President.		E. F. Howes, Treasurer.

At the stockholders' meeting held in January, 1886, most of the directors were re-elected and also the officers, with the exception of secretary, which office was filled by the election by the Board of Directors of D. E. Miles to succeed Mr. Long, who on account of ill health, resigned in December, 1885. In March, 1886, the company purchased the two-story brick building, No. 241 North Main street, the first story of which was refitted and made one of the most attractive offices in the city, and has since that time been occupied as the company's home office.

In September, 1886, President Sigler resigned and Hon. E. F. Spence was elected president of the company and Major J. R. Toberman, vice-president.

In May last the company entered Illinois and appointed S. M. Moore & Co. to represent them in that field.

The company has done a good business and now has assets of $291,000.00 with a net surplus of $13,000.00.

The officers for 1888 are the same as those for 1887, viz.: E. F. Spence, President; J. R. Toberman, Vice-President; D. E. Miles, Secretary; and F. C. Howes, Treasurer, and the following Board of Directors: John G. Downey, J. W. Davis, Dr. J. B. Hunt, F. C Howes, Dr. Isaac Fellows, Wm. H. Perry, E. F. Spence, J. R. Toberman, Nelson Vanderlip, L. W. Dennis, D. E. Miles.

The company has agents in all the principal cities and towns in California. Its San Francisco office is at 405 California street, under the management of Mr. Jno. R. Hillman.

At a meeting of the stockholders held a short time since it was decided to increase the capital to half a million dollars, which will be done as soon as possible. The company's business has steadily increased, notwithstanding the present management is very conservative.

Hon. E. F. Spence, President Southern California Insurance Company, came to California early in the fifties, when only nineteen years old, and located at Nevada City where he was for seventeen years identified with the growth and development of that very prosperous mining town. It was in that place that he first became identified with the fire insurance business (in

E. F. SPENCE.

connection with his mercantile pursuits) as agent for several companies at that time represented by Bigelow Brothers & Flint. He afterwards represented the old Pacific, which was organized and managed by Bigelow & Ralston. Mr. Spence also represented the Connecticut Mutual Life Insurance Company. After leaving Nevada City Mr. Spence moved to San José, where he was engaged in the banking business, and was also a stockholder and local director of the Home Mutual Insurance Company at that place. Mr. Spence moved to Los Angeles in 1875, and was one of the organizers of the Commercial Bank (now the First National) and its first cashier, which position he filled for several years and until elected to the office he now holds, that of president. The bank under his management has become one of the strongest financial institutions in the State.

When the Southern California Insurance Company was organized Mr. Spence was chosen one of its directors and vice-president, and was chosen president at the time of Mr. Sigler's

The Southern California Insurance Company.

OF LOS ANGELES, CAL.

resignation, which office he has filled ever since. Mr. Spence has held several important municipal offices. He served the city as a member of the council for two years, the latter of which he was President of that body. In December, 1884, he was elected Mayor of Los Angeles and served a term of two years, doing all in his power for that fast growing city.

D. E. Miles, Secretary of the Southern California, was born at Yonkers, Westchester Co., New York, where the earlier days of his life were spent. When quite a young man, went abroad spending three years, one-half of that time at school in Germany and Switzerland, and the other half in visiting the principal countries of Europe. Returning to America he entered Claverack College, near Hudson, New York, where he graduated in June, 1871, and the following fall came to California and located at Anaheim, Los Angeles County. He went into the fire insurance business as local agent shortly after arriving in this State, and has been identified with that business ever since. In January, 1886, was elected Secretary of the Southern California Insurance Company, and at the last meeting of the stockholders of his company, was re-elected secretary for the second time and also a director of the company. He is a member of the Underwriters' Association of the Pacific. He was also a partner for several years in the firm of Miles Bros., in the grain and commission business and was one of the originators of the Los Angeles Produce Exchange and was its first vice-president. He has held several offices, among them that of Member of Council of the City of Los Angeles during the years 1884 and 1885. The latter year, viz.: 1885, he was chosen president of that body, and during the absence of the mayor was acting mayor of the city, and, as is the case with President Spence, Mr. Miles has been a prominent factor in the growth and progress of the metropolis of Southern California.

D. E. MILES.

Commercial Union Assurance Company. Ld.

OF LONDON.

FOR over a quarter of a century the Commercial Union has taken a leading place in the insurance world, having been organized in 1861. The integrity of its management and its financial solidity has forced it to the very front rank of insurance companies. The Pacific Coast branch was established in this city in June, 1870, and its popularity has steadily grown during the seventeen years it has been with our people. Its liberal dealings with those who have had business relations with it, its fair adjustments and prompt payment of losses, together with its broad views on all commercial questions and its capital of $12,500,000, have made it a most popular company.

Strong, liberal and prompt, amply able to meet all its liabilities, it offers to its many patrons the following reasons why property owners should insure with them:

1st. It has been doing business on the Pacific Coast for the last twenty years.

2d. It avoids litigation and technicalities, and has no unpaid or disputed claims on the Coast.

3d. It has cash assets of $12,476,165, of which $4,222,348 is surplus to policy holders.

4th. Being possessed of such large resources at home, the company has created a Board of Trustees in New York, composed of representative American gentlemen, who now hold, in connection with various other state officers of insurance departments, the sum of $2,596,314 in trust as special security for United States policy holders, in addition to funds at the head office.

5th. Its cash income in 1886 of $5,873,365.50, gives the strongest evidence of its popularity, and the confidence of the public.

6th. It pays its losses in cash, without discount, not taking the usual 60 days.

7th. It has paid for losses over fifty-one million dollars, equal to ninety-four tons weight in United States gold coin.

The manager of the Pacific Coast branch is C. F. Mullins. His first experience in the insurance business was gained as clerk in the New York offices of the Commercial Union,

INTERIOR COMMERCIAL UNION ASSURANCE CO'S. OFFICE.

where he remained for nine years, rising rapidly to the superintendency of agencies, and later to the important post of assistant manager. When the Western branch was created in Chicago, Ill., in 1878, Mr. Mullins was selected to establish the same, and for six years as resident Secretary, he so managed the branch as to cause its business to grow apace and become prosperous. In 1884 he was transferred to the branch in this city and under his energetic and intelligent management the Commercial Union's business on this slope has steadily grown. Mr. Mullins holds high rank as an underwriter and in the special field of directing agents in the prosecution of their duties he is particularly successful.

Butler & Haldan's Agency.

REPRESENTING four prominent insurance companies of the world as general Pacific Coast agents, viz: Phenix Assurance Co. of London, American Fire Insurance Co. of New York, Western Assurance Co. of Toronto, United States Fire Insurance Co. of New York, whose aggregated capital or cash assets amount to *over ten and a quarter million dollars*, it goes without saying that the firm of Butler & Haldan ranks very high in Insurance circles on this Coast. The oldest company represented by them is the Phenix Assurance Company of London, England, which was organized in 1782, and has for more than a hundred years maintained unimpaired a high standard among insurance companies. During its long and honorable life, it has seen many of its pretentious rivals fall by the wayside; but conducting its business upon a high plane of commercial integrity, it has withstood all the storms, and landed safely upon "solid worth." The American Fire Insurance Co. of New York offers also to patrons absolute security for all risks it undertakes, and during its thirty years of life has never failed to pay its policies in full. The same can be said of the Western Assurance Co. of Toronto and the United States Fire Insurance Co. of New York, both of which offer to policy holders the utmost security.

The firm of Butler & Haldan, which represents these sterling companies as general agents for the Pacific Coast, consists of George E. Butler and E. B. Haldan. The former was for a number of years a trusted employé of the Union Insurance Co., and was afterwards the manager of the Insurance department of Cross & Co.'s business. As an underwriter of care and experience, he ranks among the foremost on this Coast, and the position he occupies in the Insurance world today is but a just tribute to his merit. Mr. Haldan entered the business on this Coast in Cross & Co's Insurance department, and there soon established the fact that underwriting was his special forte, and that he would soon hold a front place in the profession. His uniform courtesy and politeness has made him popular both in and out of business circles. In 1879 the firm was organized, and since that date has steadily advanced the business intrusted to them. They have agencies established all over this Coast, and by prompt and satisfactory adjustments of all losses, have added greatly to the already enviable reputation of the companies they represent.

Brown, Craig & Co's. Agency.

PHENIX INSURANCE COMPANY,

OF BROOKLYN, N. Y.

DATING its business life from 1853, this well known and reliable company commenced business on this Coast August 25th, 1864, and has paid out losses amounting to nearly $30,000,000 since its organization. The assets of the Company December 31st, 1886, amounted to $5,384,172 and the surplus to policy holders to $1,557,087. The great and growing popularity of the Phenix is shown in the fact that its premium income for 1886 *exceeded by nearly two million dollars that of any other company doing business in America.* The following table will give the reader an idea of its rapid and steady growth:

	Assets.	Income.
1880	$2,538,259	$2,182,977
1881	2,826,873	2,069,028
1882	3,295,327	2,496,610
1883	3,739,035	3,112,377
1884	4,342,430	4,306,410
1885	4,910,483	4,883,962
1886	5,383,172	5,333,876

The Pacific Coast branch of the Company has done its share towards this result and among insurers it to-day occupies a front place.

AMERICAN FIRE INSURANCE COMPANY,

OF PHILADELPHIA.

The American is one of the very oldest insurance organizations in the United States. It was incorporated February 28th, 1810, and commenced business March 12th, the same year, with a capital of $500,000. Its first President was Captain William Jones, who was Secretary of the Navy under President Madison. Its paid up cash capital is $500,000, its assets aggregate $2,301,856.66, and its surplus to policy holders $1,052,874.22. The Company's losses in the Boston fire in 1872 amounted to $457,801, and this large amount was as promptly paid as one tenth of the amount would have been.

PENNSYLVANIA FIRE INSURANCE COMPANY,

OF PHILADELPHIA.

The name and standing of this Company are of the highest order. It was organized in 1825 and for over sixty-two years has conducted its business upon a high plane of integrity. Its capital is $400,000 and its assets $2,710,884.92, while its surplus to policy holders amounts to $1,627,426.52, while the face value of its stock is but $100 per share, its market value is $397 per share and book value $406. This is certainly a good showing and one that must impress those desiring insurance.

Brown, Craig & Co's Agency.

THE INSURANCE COMPANY OF THE STATE OF PENNSYLVANIA.

This company was organized in 1794, and for nearly one hundred years has been known and respected as a conservative and solid organization. We, of San Francisco, whose history covers less than forty years, can hardly realize that when this city was a scattering settlement of adobe huts and fluttering sails, this company was already fifty years of age. Yet such is the fact and like good wine it has improved with age. Its assets amount to $637,538.02 and its surplus to policy holders to $392,039.78. Quiet and responsible, this company faithfully carries out all its contracts and promptly pays all its losses.

BROWN, CRAIG & CO.

Edward Brown and Homer A. Craig are the general Pacific Coast agents of the above four companies. They have subagents in all the important cities and towns of this and adjoining States and Territories, and that they are well posted and reliable underwriters is evident from the fact that they represent four of the leading insurance corporations in America. The general agency is located at No. 429 California street, San Francisco.

The Insurance Commissioner's report shows that the business of this agency was exceeded in volume in 1886 by that of only one other office. It is still growing.

Dornin & Sexton's Agency.

A strong combination of English and American insurance capital is represented at 215 Sansome street, under the management of Geo. D. Dornin and William Sexton. These embrace the following leading companies:

THE LION FIRE INSURANCE COMPANY.

This vigorous aspirant is, as its name implies, of English origin. Organized in 1879 with a guaranteed capital of $5,000,000. It was admitted to California in 1880; had on the first of January, 1887, capital and assets of $4,694,993. The management was transferred to Mr. Dornin in July, 1881, and has been rapidly advanced until its premium income ranks it among the leaders on Coast business.

THE IMPERIAL FIRE INSURANCE COMPANY,

OF LONDON.

With an organization dating back to the first years of the present century, a paid up capital of $3,000,000, and assets of $9,581,953, has enjoyed over a quarter of a century of popular patronage on the Pacific Coast. The Imperial was placed under its present managers in September, 1886, and its rapid increase of business shows the popular favor which it holds among agents, and the well applied tact and energy of the management.

THE ORIENT INSURANCE COMPANY,

OF HARTFORD,

Has $1,000,000 of paid up capital, and assets amounting to $1,551,953.68. Organized in 1867 the Orient enjoys the worldwide prestige which attaches to Hartford Insurance companies.

THE NATIONAL FIRE INSURANCE COMPANY.

OF HARTFORD.

This millionaire company succeeds the Washington Fire and Marine Insurance Company of Boston, which retired from business in January, necessitated the re-insurance of its current risks. The latter, in its Pacific department aggregated $85,000 in 1887, with the low loss rates of 41 per cent., a handsome "plum" for the National. It has a paid up capital of $1,000,000, and assets on the 1st January last of $2,006,857.34.

The coincidence will be noted that the initials of the Lion, Imperial, Orient and National form the word "Lion," the pioneer company of this agency.

This quartette of companies is under the management of Geo. D. Dornin. A pioneer of '49, he has experienced all the vicissitudes of a life during the formative period of our golden State.

His insurance record dates from 1863, when he was placed in commission as local agent for the old Phœnix, of Hartford, in an interior mining town; after four years of service he was appointed special agent and adjuster for the same company, necessitating his removal to San Francisco. In the spring of 1871 he was tendered and accepted the position of General Agent for the Fireman's Fund Insurance Company, in which capacity he rendered important service in extricating the company from the disasters which it shared with many other staunch companies in the Chicago and Boston fires.

Mr. Dornin was subsequently elected Secretary of the Fireman's Fund, retaining the position until the summer of 1881, when he resigned to accept the management of the Pacific department of the Lion Fire Insurance Company.

In 1865 Mr. Dornin was elected a member of the Assembly

from Nevada county, and again in 1867, during which session the exciting insurance legislation imposed great responsibility upon him, his well-known reputation as an underwriter giving to

GEO. D. DORNIN.

his views and opinions great weight among his fellow-legislators.

The growth of the Lion's business brought about the accession of the Orient in the fall of 1883, the Washington in 1884, and in 1886 an invitation from the Imperial head office to visit London to arrange for the transfer of the Pacific department of that important company. The revenue of Mr. Dornin's department for 1887 reached over $400,000.

William Sexton was also a member of the California Legislature (from Placer county) in the session of 1865, and the intimacy then formed between these gentlemen during that session has continued uninterruptedly ever since. Mr. Sexton received his first commission as an insurance agent for San Jose from Mr. Dornin for the Fireman's Fund in 1868, was subsequently promoted to general agent, and resigned in 1881 to accept the assistant manager's position for the Lion with Mr. Dornin. Mr. Sexton's specialty as an adjuster ranks him among the leaders on the Coast. Added to a genial *bonhomie* manner, he has a rare knowledge of men and motives, and a degree of tact and patience, which enables him to dispose of knotty problems in adjustments, so as to leave claimant and company equally well satisfied. Few men in the profession are more welcome in their local agent's offices than William Sexton.

The territory, under the jurisdiction of these gentlemen, embraces the whole Pacific Coast and the Hawaiian Kingdom.

Their field work is supervised by Special Agents Volney Howard, John H. Clinkscales and B. B. Broomell. In addition to these the office staff numbers twenty, the growth of the business necessitates enlarged office accommodations, for which a lease has been secured of the lower story and basement of the

WILLIAM SEXTON.

elegant new building now in course of erection opposite their present office. The spacious rooms will be especially fitted up for their requirements, and ready for occupancy by July 1st.

HOME INSURANCE COMPANY,

OF NEW YORK.

GREAT and prosperous as a corporation, and popular in every State and Territory of America is the reputation of the Home, of New York, which was organized in 1853, and commenced to write insurance on this Coast in 1856. Prudent, skillful, and energetic management, and the unwavering policy of strict business integrity, have made the Home, of New York, a continual success, until its cash assets on the July 1st, 1887, reached the large item of $7,855,509.62. This includes a paid up capital of $3,000,000, a reserve premium fund of $3,108,596, in addition to $304,419.04 reserved for unpaid losses and claims, leaving a net surplus of $1,442,494.58. These figures are sufficient to show that the Home, of New York, has gained the confidence and esteem of the community at large, and are the best evidence that its operations are conducted on a sound and equitable basis.

The Home, of New York, is one of those progressive institutions in which Americans may feel some national pride. With a clear and brilliant record of thirty-four years, it now stands in the foremost rank in point of financial strength, business standing and powerful influence, having outrivaled all its older American competitors. It has well earned the universal confidence which it now enjoys, and deserves unlimited patronage.

The Pacific Department of the Home, of New York, (in addition to the Phœnix, of Hartford) has, since 1874, been under the careful direction of Captain Arthur E. Magill, and with his executive ability, it has the same unqualified success throughout the Pacific Coast it enjoys in the Eastern States.

THE PHŒNIX INSURANCE COMPANY,

OF HARTFORD, CONN.

The Phœnix Insurance Company, of Hartford, Conn., was organized in June, 1854, and began business on the Pacific Coast in 1857. Its career has been one of steady and sterling progress, owing to its conservative and efficient management, with scrupulous fidelity to honorable methods and promptness in paying losses. The Phœnix, of Hartford, suffered severely in the Chicago conflagration of 1871, but promptly paid all claims in full, amounting to nearly a million dollars. It again sustained enormous losses in the year following by the Boston conflagration, but again proved itself equal to the occasion, paying every dollar of liability. The fact that the Phœnix, of Hartford, passed so triumphantly through the fiery ordeal of these two years, to say nothing of the financial vicissitudes, confirms its merits and character as a true insurance company, and has made it renowned as one of those solid, popular and progressive corporations on which the public may rely with complete confidence.

The gross assets of the Phœnix, of Hartford, on July 1st, 1887, amounted to $4,737,669.52, of which $2,000,000 represents capital stock fully paid up, $1,469,814.11 being a reserved

CAPTAIN ARTHUR E. MAGILL.

premium fund, and $174,330.90 reserved for unsettled losses, leaving a net surplus of $1,093,524.51.

Captain Arthur E. Magill has had the care of the Pacific Branch of the Phœnix, of Hartford (in addition to the Home, of New York,) since 1874, and it is almost needless to say, that in his hands, the affairs of the company on this Coast have been exceedingly prosperous.

Captain Arthur E. Magill, the general agent, (Pacific Department) of the Home and Phœnix Insurance Companies, is well known and regarded as a thoroughly experienced and prudent underwriter. His energy and devotion to the details of his profession, his honorable principles, and invariable courtesy, have won for him and his companies an enviable reputation. That he is well esteemed by those who best know him may be inferred from the fact that he holds the responsible position of President

Captain Arthur E. Magill's Agency.

of the Pacific Insurance Union, which comprises within its membership all the representative underwriters of the Pacific Coast. [A full account of this important and influential organization will be found on another page of this work.] Captain Arthur E. Magill, as general agent of the Home, of New York, and the Phœnix, of Hartford, has the superintendence of a wide range of territory, including California, Oregon, Nevada, Idaho, Washington, Montana, Utah, and Arizona, and over three hundred agencies report to his general agency office in San Francisco.

The Home and the Phœnix, though separate and distinct companies, became in 1886, associated in the Pacific Department under one management, and have since issued joint policies, by which each company assumes half the total liability, thus making a strong combination.

Staunch companies like these, while managed with such probity, enterprise and care, cannot fail to maintain the increasing patronage of those who seek reliable indemnity against loss by fire, their patrons being satisfied that should loss occur their claims will be adjusted and paid with all reasonable dispatch and impartial fairness.

Balfour, Guthrie & Co's. Agency.

BRITISH AND FOREIGN MARINE INSURANCE CO.,

OF LIVERPOOL.

PROMINENT among the Marine Insurance corporations of the world stands the British and Foreign Marine Insurance Company. Its paid up cash capital is $960,000, while its assets reach $4,534,142.07 against which its liabilities amount to the sum of only $758,102.06. It will be seen from this statement that its surplus over all liabilities including capital stock amounts to $2,816,040.01. Certainly owners and shippers should feel satisfied that a policy written by this solid company was a sure safeguard against loss.

LONDON AND LANCASHIRE FIRE INSURANCE CO.,

OF LIVERPOOL.

This is a name that has become familiar all over the world. The company was organized in 1861, and for twenty-seven years it has steadily grown in public favor. The company has a paid up capital of $926,000, and assets of $3,262,590.71, and an annual income of two and a half millions of dollars. Its business life on this Coast commenced many years ago, and no company doing business in this section has made a better record than the London and Lancashire.

CALEDONIAN INSURANCE COMPANY,

OF EDINBURGH.

The Caledonian Insurance Company is the oldest insurance corporation in Scotland, it having been incorporated in 1805, and has so grown as to show for the year 1886 assets amounting to nearly $2,000,000 and an income of $671,992.69. Although it has been represented on this Coast for but two years its course has been such as to commend it to property owners and business men throughout this section.

MANCHESTER INSURANCE COMPANY,

OF MANCHESTER.

This company has a subscribed capital of $5,000,000, of which $500,000 is paid up, and assets amounting to $1,324,067.50, while its income for 1886 amounted to $1,261,852.50. It was organized in 1824 and has a clean and honest record of over a half century. The company was admitted to this State in 1880, and soon took a front place in insurance circles, which it has since maintained.

AMERICAN INSURANCE COMPANY,

OF NEWARK, N. J.

In all the essentials that characterize representative fire underwriting corporations, the American Insurance Company is unsurpassed. It was organized in 1846, and since that date it has been continuously and honestly engaged in the business of furnishing indemnity against loss by fire, and its record, so full of success and honor, forms an important part of the insurance history of the country.

The financial condition of the company, briefly expressed, as shown by the official reports of the Insurance Commissioner for 1886, is as follows: paid up cash capital, $600,000; gross assets, $1,848,314.86; and net surplus, $902,049.88. The range of its general business account is thus indicated: amount of net profits received during the year, $390,106.90; total income for the year, $466,673.34; total amount paid for losses during the year 1886, $165,166.02; paid out in dividends, $67,160.20.

BALFOUR, GUTHRIE & CO., GENERAL AGENTS.

The firm of Balfour, Guthrie & Co., the General Agents of the above companies is one of the largest shipping and commis-

Balfour, Guthrie & Co's Agency.

sion firms in the world. The several names of their houses are as follows: Balfour, Williamson & Co., Liverpool; Balfour, Guthrie & Co., San Francisco; Balfour, Guthrie & Co., Portland; Williamson, Balfour & Co., Valparaiso. The reputation of the firm extends to every country visited by the ships of the world.

The management of the insurance business of this firm is in the hands of Geo. W. Spencer, who as an underwriter, ranks well among insurance men on this Coast. Mr. Spencer's thorough familiarity with all the details of both fire and marine underwriting, and the business-like manner in which he handles the many sub-agents of his companies, leave no doubt as to his ability, and that he is the "right man in the right place" is universally acknowledged.

H. M. Newhall & Co's. Agency.

KNOWN wherever the trade of San Francisco goes the firm of H. M. Newhall & Co., in addition to their large shipping and commission business, represent as General Agents three of the large foreign and eastern insurance companies.

NATIONAL ASSURANCE COMPANY,

OF IRELAND,

Is the only Irish company represented in the United States. This company was organized under the laws of Great Britain and Ireland in 1823, with a subscribed capital of $5,000,000, of which $500,000 was paid up. At the close of 1886, its assets amounted to $2,806,097, with liabilities inclusive of unearned premiums of $1,907,730, showing a surplus of $898,367, its business for that year was $898,367, its losses paid were $566,065. The National of Ireland began business on this Coast in 1885, H. M. Newhall & Co., being appointed General Agents.

THE ATLAS ASSURANCE COMPANY,

OF LONDON.

This company, doing a Fire and Life Insurance business, was incorporated in London, England, in 1808, with a subscribed capital of $6,000,000, of which $720,000 was paid up. It has done a most successful business, for at the close of 1886 its assets amounted to the large sum of $8,770,212.05, with liabilities including unearned premiums $7,517,327.20, showing a net surplus of $1,252,884.85. Its income for 1886 amounted to $706,868.95, while its total premiums received since organization reached the sum of $21,595,285, while its losses amounted to $14,786,544. The company has done a successful business on this Coast, and ranks with the best of the old English companies. It commenced business on this Coast in 1886, with H. M. Newhall & Co., General Agents.

THE BOYLSTON INSURANCE COMPANY.

OF BOSTON, MASS.

To those desiring American indemnity this company offers unusual advantages. It ranks among the solid institutions of the wealthy city of Boston, incorporated in 1872 with a capital

A. R. GURRY.

H. M. Newhall & Co's. Agency.

of $557,200, all paid up. It has assets now of $916,520.79, with liabilities of $187,859.11, showing a net surplus on capital and liabilities of $171,261.68. Its income for 1886 was $306,-133.94, and its premium receipts since organization have been $5,019,676.62; it has paid losses since its organization to the amount of $3,006,953.58.

H. M. Newhall & Co., secured in May last, the services of A. R. Gurrey, whose long experience as special agent for English companies on this Coast well fitted him for the responsible position which he now fills as manager of the insurance department. H. M. Newhall & Co., offer to those desiring insurance on this Coast three nationalities, English, Irish and American, and the companies represented are solid, old and reliable, doing business on a liberal basis, settling all losses promptly and justly, and offering advantages second to none and showing combined assets of $12,492,629.84.

The Thames and Mersey.

MARINE Insurance Company, (Limited) of Liverpool, London and Manchester, though not so old as some of its cotemporary companies in England, nevertheless stands high both at home and abroad, alike for its financial solidity and its integrity of management. It was organized in 1860, and thus has a record of nearly thirty years, to which it is able to point with gratification and pride. It has a subscribed capital of $10,000,000, a paid up capital of $1,000,-000 and its total assets as reported July 1, 1887, were $5,809,629. It is the largest strictly marine company in the world, and is known in every seaport. The company has made a fine record for liberality; particularly has it shown its good judgment as well as generosity by rewarding in a substantial manner shipmasters who have shown unusual skill or bravery in protecting the property under their charge in trying occasions. Wm. Greer Harrison, one of the best known and most popular of San Francisco's underwriters, has had the management of the Pacific Coast department of the company for many years. He occupies a prominent position in social and business circles and, beside several other positions of influence, is President of the Association of Marine Underwriters. A sketch of that organization together with the picture of its president is given on another page. Recently the office was moved to the block on the corner of Battery and California streets, which has of late become quite an insurance center. A picture of the office is presented here. The Thames and Mersey has the lion's share of the insurance on wheat cargoes from this port, but does a large business in other directions as well.

The scope of the company is seen by a glance at the location of the principal agencies which are at Antwerp, Rotterdam, Amsterdam, Bremen, Hamburg, Paris, Havre, Marseilles, Calcutta, Colombo, Singapore, Madras, Bombay, Penang, Foochow, Hankow, Hongkong, Shanghai, Rangoon, Yokohama, Wellington, N. Z., with sub-agencies at all the principal New Zealand ports; Melbourne and sub-agencies at Australian ports; New York, with correspondents at all Atlantic ports of the United States and Canada; San Francisco with sub-agencies at Portland and Victoria; Valparaiso and Lima.

THE THAMES & MERSEY INS. CO.'S OFFICE.

Gutte & Frank's Agency.

PACIFIC Coast managers for Germania Fire Insurance Company, of New York; Magdeburg Fire Insurance Company, of Magdeburg; Hamburg; Magdeburg Fire Insurance Company, of Hamburg-Magdeburg General (Marine) Insurance Company, of Magdeburg; National Marine Insurance Association, of London; Economic Fire Office, of London; and Franco-Hungarian Insurance Company (Marine), of Budapest.

Heading this article is a list of sterling and reliable fire and marine companies which is sufficient to justify the assertion that the firm of Gutte & Frank ranks among the foremost in insurance circles on this Coast.

The firm of Gutte & Frank has been in existence since 1876, having that year been appointed Pacific Coast managers of the Hamburg-Mngdeburg Fire Insurance Company, of Hamburg, and since that date they have added the other companies, until at this time they represent one of the strongest general agencies on the Pacific. The Magdeburg Fire Insurance Company, of Magdeburg, alone has during its business life paid out in losses over *sixty millions of dollars*, and during the same period has received in premiums some *ninety-seven millions of dollars*. The record of the other companies represented by these gentlemen is just as clean and shows the same safe conservative management as does the old Magdeburg. The firm of Gutte & Frank consists of Isidor Gutte and William Frank, and their reputation as competent painstaking underwriters and reliable, honorable business men is such as to make their agency popular with all classes of insurers. Mr. Gutte has lived in San Francisco for many years, and before connecting himself with Mr. Frank was engaged in the shipping and commission business. He is generally regarded as one of our most public-spirited citizens, and has always been foremost in matters of public good. He is prominent in aquatic circles, and is Commodore of the San Francisco Yacht Club. In insurance circles Mr. Gutte has long been a leading spirit and enjoys alike the confidence and esteem of insurers and insured. Mr. William Frank's connection with underwriting dates from 1869, when he started as an insurance broker and so continued until 1876 when he associated himself with Mr. Gutte. Mr. Frank has thoroughly mastered the insurance business in all its various branches, and by his energy and experience become one of our most reliable underwriters. Before engaging in the insurance business he was for a number of years an importer in this city, and had earned an excellent reputation as an upright business man. The firm's territory extends from the Rocky Mountains to the Pacific Ocean, and their agents are to be found in every town and city west of the Rockies. The well-known character of the managers, and the solid financial standing of the companies represented by them, combine to make it the interest of those desiring policies *that do insure* to see that their risks are placed in some one of the companies referred to above.

Ætna Insurance Company

OF HARTFORD.

JUSTLY prominent among the foremost insurance companies represented on this Coast, is the old reliable "Ætna of Hartford." The Company was organized in 1819, and established its Pacific Coast business thirty years ago. The branch or general agency here covers all the States and Territories of the Union west of the Rocky Mountains, as well as British Columbia and the Hawaiian Islands. The capital (which is all paid up) amounts to $4,000,000, and the net surplus to $3,450,221.37. Since its organization this solid company has paid out in losses to property owners $60,180,618.19, including the sum of $3,780,000 in Chicago in 1870, and $1,600,000 in Boston, 1871. Nowhere in the history of this company can there be found a single instance in which they have failed to promptly meet all losses and the reputation of the company for the prompt and satisfactory adjustment of claims is certainly enviable.

The Ætna having the largest capital and largest surplus of any company in America, is the strongest and one of the most reliable doing business on this Coast.

The general agent of the company here is Geo. C. Boardman, who has occupied this important post since 1868. Mr. Boardman first located in San Francisco in 1860 as special agent of a Hartford company, by whom he had been employed for several years. In 1861, he assisted in organizing the San Francisco Insurance Company, and became its Secretary and shortly afterwards was elected President of the Company, which position he retained until 1868, when he resigned to accept the general agency of the Ætna of Hartford. Later in the same year, the San Francisco retired from business, re-assuring its risks in the Liverpool & London & Globe, and returning to its stockholders the capital and a handsome surplus, which represented the profits of its business.

Mr. Boardman is ably assisted in the management of the general agency by T. E. Pope. This branch employs eleven clerks and seven solicitors. With an underwriting experience of over a quarter of a century, it is useless to say that in insurance circles Mr. Boardman occupies a prominent place

Jacobs & Easton's Agency.

Very Truly Yours
Julius Jacobs

REPRESENT locally the Insurance Company of North America, and are Pacific Department Managers of the Springfield, Merchants of Newark, N. J., Glens Falls, Union, Howard, Concordia, Merchants of w York, Clinton Insurance Company of Dakota, and the ociate Managers of the Fire Insurance Association of Lon-i, in which latter management they have associated with them . W. L. Chalmers, a well-known underwriter, and for many rs the company's special agent on the Pacific Coast.

The present firm consisting of Julius Jacobs and George Easton, was organized in November, 1878, succeeding the firm of Potter, Jacobs & Easton, which latter firm was formed some four years prior. Both Messrs. Jacobs and Easton began their insurance career here many years ago, the former in 1860 and the latter in 1867, both at the latter date being connected

Very truly Yours
Geo. Easton

with the general agency of the North British and Mercantile.

In '69 and '70 both gentlemen were connected with the Occidental Insurance Company a prominent local, the senior as general agent and the junior in clerical capacity in the office of the company, which, owing to the vicissitudes of the Chicago fire, was compelled to wind up, though prior to that time Mr. Jacobs had been the General Agent of the Cleveland Insurance Company, which general agency he held at the time of the Chicago fire. Though drifting apart then for a time Messrs. Jacobs and Easton finally formed a coalition in 1874 which partnership has been continued uninterruptedly to date.

The growth of the business of the present firm, as shown by the statistics we have been permitted to peruse, is somewhat phenomenal, and is evidence of what close attention to duty and earnest endeavor to please will accomplish in underwriting circles. The firm's business in 1878 aggregated about $40,000, while the year just closed shows it has increased to more than tenfold, and that an increase has been gradual and continuous from year to year is evidence of constant and earnest application.

Julius Jacobs enjoys the distinction of being one of the Pioneer underwriters of the Pacific Slope, having taken his first risk in California in 1860 as agent, at Folsom, California, of the North British and Mercantile Insurance Company. Later he became a partner in the firm of Gridley, Hobart and Jacobs of Austin, Nevada, and Folsom, California, he being in charge of the Folsom business. This firm was specially known in early days both on account of its extended trade and on account of the famous sack of flour which has made the name of Mr. Gridley historical and yielded for the sanitary fund nearly $200,000. In 1866 Mr. Jacobs removed to this city and retiring from mercantile business has since devoted himself to the profession of insurance.

It is needless to add that with a handsome and eligibly located office, conveniently and comfortably arranged, as shown in the accompanying cut, with a corps of efficient and intelligent assistants the office presents a favorable inducement, and as worthy of patronage as any on the street, and particularly representing as it does the strongest combination of companies in any single general agency in the United States, and Jacobs & Easton are to be congratulated, upon the successful showing they make, and the companies as well, in securing the continued services of such worthy representatives.

INTERIOR JACOBS & EASTON'S OFFICE.

North British and Mercantile Insurance Company

OF LONDON AND EDINBURGH.

NORTH British, as it is popularly known, has a long and honorable record, both at home and in this country. It was incorporated under royal charter in 1809, and commenced business on the Pacific Coast in 1861. Its career on this coast has been so eminently creditable as to render it exceedingly popular among all classes of owners. Steady prosperity has been the result and to-day no company doing business in this section has a better reputation among merchants and property owners. Its capital is fifteen million dollars, and of its total assets as shown by the official report for January 1st, 1887, the sum of $11,907,289.05 is invested in unencumbered real estate, stocks, bonds, and mortgages, and the further sum of $1,949,928.53 consists of cash in bank and at branches and agencies, making its total assets $13,857,217.58, while its liabilities are but $3,067,231.06, leaving a surplus as regards policy holders of $10,789,986.52. This most creditable showing is appreciated by its many patrons and needs no comment here. It may be added however, that by a glance at the tables in the latest report of the State Insurance Commissioner, it will be seen that this company has no losses resisted and none unadjusted.

GERMAN AMERICAN INSURANCE COMPANY.

The company above named, though not so old as some of its cotemporaries, nevertheless stands high. It was incorporated in the State of New York in 1872, and was admitted to do business on this Coast in October, 1873. The official statement of this company dated January 1st, 1887, is as follows:

ASSETS.

United States Bonds	$2,711,025.00
Other Stocks and Bonds	2,194,640.00
Cash on hand and agency balances	245,234.03
Total Assets	$5,150,899.03
Total Liabilities	1,806,625.89
Surplus as regards policy holders	$3,344,273.14

In furnishing indemnity against loss by fire, the history of this company, so full of success and honor, forms an important part in the insurance history of this Coast and its popularity is fully merited. Tom C. Grant is the Pacific Coast manager of these important companies.

Hartford Fire Insurance Company,

OF HARTFORD, CONN.

COMMENCING business in this State in January, 1870, this staunch and reliable company, which was organized in 1794, has rapidly gained friends. The Pacific Coast Department, which is under the management of Belden & Cofran, embraces the following States and Territories: California, Oregon, Washington, Idaho, Nevada, Montana, Utah, Arizona, British Columbia and the Hawaiian Islands. That this department is well managed by the gentlemen in charge is evidenced by the popularity enjoyed by the company throughout the Coast. The solid financial standing of the Hartford, and equitable manner in which it has adjusted all its losses during a career of nearly one hundred years, has caused it to be sought by property owners who desire to secure a policy *that does insure*. The following annual statement, issued January 1st, 1887, will be of interest to insurers:

ASSETS.

Cash on hand, in Bank and Cash Items	$ 366,830 75
Cash in hands of Agents and in course of Transmission	339,942 74
Rents and accrued Interest	28,861 86
Real Estate Unencumbered	653,575 60
Loans on Bond and Mortgage (1st lien)	$1,173,900 00
Loans on Collateral Security	60,000 00
Bank Stock, Hartford, Market Value	323,847 00
" New York, "	241,300 00
" Boston, "	77,957 50
" Albany and Montreal, Market Value	87,010 00
Railroad Stocks	454,310 00
State, City and Railroad Bonds	906,700 00
United States Bonds	226,525 00
Total	$5,035,946 45
Cash Capital	$1,250,000 00
Reserve for Re-Insurance (legal standard)	1,764,932 23
Outstanding Claims	231,027 45
Policy Holders' Surplus	3,039,956 74

It will be seen from the above statement that the surplus as regards property holders amounts to over $3,000,000. With the help of their many agents throughout the western country, and the well posted clerks in their office here, Belden & Cofran are enabled to handle large lines of insurance with promptness and dispatch. Throughout this entire section the name of the Hartford has become a househould word, and owners find it advantageous to secure their policies with this company.

Guardian Assurance Company,

OF LONDON.

THIS sterling English company was organized in 1821, and has for a number of years ranked among the foremost companies of the world. It has a capital stock of $5,000,000, and its annual statement issued January 1, 1887, shows its assets to be $20,617,292.37, while its liabilities reach $12,823,077.32. The United States department report for the year ending December 31, 1887, shows that the aggregate amount of assets of the company in this country is $1,391,924.49, while the total amount of liabilities is but $598,558.23, leaving a surplus beyond all liabilities in the United States alone of $793,365.96. The gross premiums on risks written and renewed during the year 1887 in the United

WM. J. LANDERS.

States, was $881,268.94, and of this amount the Pacific Coast branch furnished its full share.

The average loss percentage of the Pacific Coast business of the Guardian for the past ten years was 35.75, which is materially less than any of its competitors, and is a high tribute to the efficient and conservative management of its General Agent, Wm. J. Landers.

Mr. Landers was born in the city of Brooklyn, New York, in the year 1851, and came to the Pacific Coast in 1869, and has since been continually engaged in the business of fire insurance. He commenced as junior clerk in the office of the Oriental Insurance Company of San Francisco, the late Jno. R. Hamilton being the only other clerk, and upon the company retiring from business, after a short existence of about nine months, Mr. Landers went into the employ of the San Francisco agency of the Lorillard Insurance Company of New York. Upon the forced retirement of this Company, by reason of the Chicago fire in 1871, he at once entered the employ of Falkner, Bell & Co., representing the Imperial of London, and later on the Queen of Liverpool, first as policy writer and counter clerk, and then as special agent and adjuster, serving in the latter capacity for about three years, succeeding Mr. Van Dyke Hubbard.

In December, 1876, the Guardian Assurance Company of London opened an agency upon the Pacific Coast, and Mr. Landers accepted the position of manager under Balfour, Guthrie & Co., General Agents. This position he held until late in 1879, when he was appointed General Agent for the Pacific Coast, and has acted in that capacity for the Company during the last nine years.

The earlier experience of Mr. Landers was at a time when chaos reigned as to rates and commissions, and covering the intervening years of the Board of Fire Underwriters and Pacific Insurance Union, it will be seen that he is well versed in the ups and downs of the business.

He caused the first insurance maps to be made of the canneries upon the Columbia River, and made a special study of this and other classes of special hazards, contributing from time to time articles upon the physical hazard to the underwriting press; he also associated a few offices with his own, and originated the survey and publication of the well known grain warehouse diagrams now in general use in the offices and banks.

From time to time he has served upon the more important committees of the Board of Fire Underwriters and Pacific Insurance Union, the formation and constitution of the latter as originally adopted resulting from the work of a committee of which he was an active member; he has also served for some years as Director, Secretary and Treasurer of the San Francisco Fire Patrol and as a member of the committee in charge of the Inspection Bureau.

Mr. Landers is well known outside of insurance circles, and is considerably interested in real estate in Alameda, Santa Clara, Sacramento and San Francisco counties. He resides at San Leandro, in Alameda county, where his home is one of the most attractive of the many beautiful residences to be found there.

Westchester Fire Insurance Company.

OF NEW YORK.

ON March 14th, 1837, the legislature of the State of New York passed an act, the first section of which read as follows:

"James Burlin et als, and all other persons who may hereafter associate with them in the manner herein proscribed, shall be a corporation by the name of The Westchester County Mutual Insurance Company for the purpose of insuring their respective dwelling houses, stores, shops, and other buildings against loss or damage by fire."

A. C. DONNELL.

This new corporation had for its home the village of New Rochelle, Westchester County, New York.

The company was changed from a mutual to a joint stock company, August 11, 1869, and the name altered to the Westchester Fire Insurance Company.

In March, 1883, it removed its principal office from New Rochelle to the city of New York, and has since been an ambitious and conspicuous corporation among the leading fire companies at the metropolis. Its annual statement shows assets of $1,304,126.90, net surplus $310,510.68, and an income of $946,409.20.

The Westchester is represented in this field by A. C. Donnell, whose jurisdiction extends over California, Nevada, Arizona, Utah and Washington Territory.

Mr. Donnell is also manager for the San Francisco Department of the California Insurance Company, and the Union of New Zealand.

Mr. Donnell controls a very handsome city business, his city premiums amounting to nearly $80,000 for his three companies. Under his able and energetic management of the Pacific Department the Westchester has attained a prominent place with its competitors.

Agents have been appointed in all the prominent cities, towns and villages, and by present indications the company can congratulate itself on a prosperous future. The following statement of its affairs was issued January 1st:

CAPITAL STOCK—PAID IN, $300,000.00.

ASSETS.

	Market Value.
U. S. 4 per cent. Bonds	$ 383,000.00
Bonds and Mortgages	249,250.00
Albany & Susquehanna R. R. Stock	57,600.00
N. Y. & Harlem R. R. Stock	112,500.00
Rensselaer & Saratoga R. R. Stock	85,000.00
N. Y., Lackawanna & Western R. R. Stock	52,500.00
Northern Pacific R. R. Bonds	23,800.00
Missouri, Kansas & Texas R. R. Bonds	20,000.00
Missouri Pacific R. R. Bonds	23,000.00
Oregon Short Line R. R. Bonds	21,500.00
St. Louis, Iron Mountain & Southern R. R. Bonds	15,000.00
N. Y. Central R. R. Bonds	10,500.00
Georgia State Bonds	22,000.00
Loans on Collaterals	51,500.00
Real Estate	2,000.00
Premiums in course of collection	92,782.88
Cash in Bank	80,106.78
Interest due and accrued	2,287.24
Total assets	$1,304,126.90

LIABILITIES.

Unpaid Losses and other Claims	$ 57,521.01	
Unearned Premiums or Re-insurance Fund	636,095.21	
Total Liabilities		$ 693,616.22
Net Surplus as regards Policy Holders		$ 610,510.68
Net Surplus as regards Stockholders		$ 310,510.68
Total Income, year 1886		$946,409.20
" Expenditures, (including 10% Dividends to stockholders		$813,885.01
Income exceeds all Expenditures for year 1886		$132,524.19

This Company has been in continuous and successful operation for a half century.

The Liverpool and London and Globe Insurance Company.

A FAMOUS organization, with an extraordinary history, is the one named above. In a word, it is recognized as the largest fire insurance company in the world, and its fame is world wide. Its gross fire assets aggregate $17,000,000 and its net surplus over $10,000,-

CHIEF OFFICE, PACIFIC DEPARTMENT,
COMPANY'S BUILDING, 422 CALIFORNIA ST., S. F.

000. The assets of the United States Branch of this great corporation, which are invested in the names of its Trustees in America for the exclusive protection of its policy holders in this country, are equaled in volume of assets by only two or three companies. The immense assets and the unlimited liability of more than thirteen hundred shareholders, make this Company one of the very best for those desiring first-class indemnity. The company was organized in 1836 and commenced business in America in 1848. Its Pacific Coast branch was established in 1852, and issued the first fire insurance policy ever written on this Coast. Its career in this country has been an experience of uninterrupted progess, despite single years of extraordinary loss, such as the great fires of 1871 and 1872 in Chicago and Boston, in which it paid losses amounting to over four and a half millions of dollars. As a proof of the company's progress in the United States, the following exhibit is interesting: The net fire premiums received in 1848, the year the American branch was established, amounted to $4,520; in 1860 they had increased to $455,775, and in 1870 to $2,114,173. At the end of another decade, the close of 1880, they showed a total for that year of $2,664,242, and during the year 1886 they reached the handsome sum of $3,686,553, thus exceeding that of any company doing business in the United States. The gross business of the company in this country since its entrance here shows an aggregate premium income of $66,445,599, and an aggregate loss payment of 39,514,898. The assets of the American branch on January 1st, 1887, including San Francisco real estate, amounted to $6,639,781, and its surplus over all liabilties $3,077,538. The business in this country is controlled by American directors absolutely. The business on this Coast is in the hands of Mr. Charles D. Haven, Resident Secretary who is ably assisted by Col. C. Mason Kinne, as Special Agent. The San Francisco directors are as follows: Wm. Alvord, President Bank of California; Levi Strauss, of Levi Strauss & Co.; William T. Coleman, of Wm. T. Coleman & Co., and William Babcock, of Parrott & Co.

Rolla V. Watt's Agency.

ROLLA V. WATT is one of the youngest general agents on the Coast, having just reached the age of thirty-one. Mr. Watt is a native of Ohio, and came to California in 1876 when he entered the employ of the general agency of the American Central Insurance Company in this city as clerk. He later became city and special agent, and in April, 1887, was appointed general agent of the Company, at the same time securing the general agency of the Amazon Insurance Company and Pacific Fire Insurance Company. In July, 1887, the Liberty Insurance Company was added to his list and he now conducts one of the most promising agencies on the Coast, and in his hands the interests of the companies are well guarded and advanced.

Mr. Watt also represents the Lloyds Plate Glass Insurance Company and is Secretary of the Pacific Investment Association, a most thriving real estate concern. He is also a Director of the Young Men's Christian Association and takes much interest in that institution, believing that the large number of young men who are migrating to this Coast should, while far away from home influences, be provided with Christian amusements.

Of the companies represented by Mr. Watt, the American Central has assets amounting to $1,258,000.84; the Amazon to $584,783.83; the Pacific Fire to $749,826.35, and the Liberty with a cash capital of $1,000,000 and large assets.

Hutchinson & Mann's Agency.

THE firm of Hutchinson & Mann, which now consists of H. R. Mann and John Scott Wilson, was established in this city in 1872, by C. I. Hutchinson, H. R. Mann and A. D. Smith, under the firm name of Hutchinson, Mann & Smith. In 1876 Mr. Smith retired and the firm name was changed to its present title. In the fall of 1884 General Hutchinson died, and in July, 1885, H. R. Mann and John Scott Wilson formed the present firm of Hutchinson & Mann, retaining the old name, owing to the excellent reputation which it had.

H. R. Mann is a native of Michigan and came to California when nine years of age. In 1869 he entered into the insurance business as local agent in Salt Lake city. Finding that field too small, he came to San Francisco in 1871, and established the firm of Hutchinson, Mann & Smith.

John Scott Wilson was born in the State of Illinois, came to San Francisco in 1854; was graduated from Kenyon College, Ohio, in 1870; engaged in mercantile business five years; was member of the San Francisco Stock and Exchange Board for many years, at one time having been president of the Exchange. In July, 1885, formed partnership with H. R. Mann, organizing the present firm.

Hutchinson & Mann are Pacific Coast agents of the following companies; their territory embracing all the States and territories west of the Rocky Mountains:

CONTINENTAL INSURANCE COMPANY,
OF NEW YORK,

Has a capital paid in of $1,000,000 and a net surplus of $1,374,000. This sterling company was organized in 1852 and has been well and favorably known on this coast since 1872. It conducts its business under the safety fund law of the State of New York. It met the demands of the large conflagrations in Chicago and Boston with 100 cents on the dollar. Its officers and directors are among the best business men of New York, and its business course is one of promptness and reliability.

THE AGRICULTURAL INSURANCE COMPANY,
OF WATERTOWN, N. Y.,

Was organized in 1853 and commenced business on this coast in 1876. It has a capital of $500,000, net assets of $1,887,330, and a net surplus of policy holders of $753,152. This company has paid out since its organization in losses, over five and one-half millions of dollars.

CITIZENS' INSURANCE COMPANY,
OF CINCINNATI, OHIO,

Is a new bidder for favors in this field. It has a capital of $200,000 and available assets reaching nearly $300,000.

ST. PAUL FIRE AND MARINE INSURANCE CO.,
OF ST. PAUL, MINN.,

Was organized in 1865 and entered this State in 1872. The company's capital is $500,000, its assets $1,541,060, and its net surplus $359,942. Its total cash income for the year 1887 was $1,070,473. This is a creditable showing and one that ought to satisfy policy holders.

FIREMEN'S INSURANCE COMPANY,
OF NEWARK, N. J.,

Has a capital of $600,000, assets of $1,688,741, and surplus to policy holders of $1,463,653. This company has the largest surplus to policy holders in proportion to assets, of any company in the world. The organization of the company dates from 1855, and its business on this coast from 1885.

OREGON FIRE AND MARINE INSURANCE COMPANY,
OF PORTLAND, OREGON,

Has an authorized capital of $300,000, of which $220,100 is paid up, and a surplus as regards policy holders of $318,671. The company was organized in 1881, and in 1884 established a branch here. It numbers in its Board of Directors some of the most prominent merchants of Oregon, and as a Pacific Coast organization it deserves success.

CITIZENS' INSURANCE COMPANY,
OF ST. LOUIS, MO.,

Is over a half century old, having been organized in 1837. Its 51st annual statement shows its capital to be $200,000, and its net surplus over all liabilities nearly $200,000. Since its entrance into this State it has been under the able management of the present agents, and is making rapid strides.

TEUTONIA INSURANCE COMPANY,
OF NEW ORLEANS, LA.,

Was organized in the Crescent City in 1864, and commenced taking risks on this coast in 1879. Its capital is $250,000 and its assets $415,667. It has paid this year two semi-annual dividends of five per cent, making ten per cent for the year.

UNITED FIRE RE-INSURANCE COMPANY,
OF MANCHESTER, ENG.,

Has in the United States assets amounting to $1,188,793, and a net surplus of $410,338. Its United States business is in charge of William Wood of New York, under whose able management the company has made rapid strides. Its board of American directors are among the most prominent men of New York business circles.

Hutchinson & Mann's Agency.

GIRARD INSURANCE COMPANY,

OF PHILADELPHIA, PA.,

Was organized in 1853 with a capital of $200,000. Its paid up capital now stands $300,000, and its assets $1,357,468, while its net surplus is $602,485. This company has been one of the most successful in the United States. Its president, A. S. Gillett, is one of the ablest business men of Philadelphia, and its directors among the most prominent men of the city.

FIREMAN'S INSURANCE COMPANY,

OF BALTIMORE, MD.,

Was organized in 1825. Its capital stock is $378,000, assets amounting to over half a million. Gen. J. M. Anderson has been president of this company for many years and its Board of Directors are among the most substantial business men of Baltimore, and with but few exceptions have held the position of directors for over twenty-five years. This sterling company is most favorably known on this Coast and does an excellent business.

SUN FIRE OFFICE,

OF LONDON, ENGLAND,

Is the oldest purely fire insurance company in the world, having been organized in 1710. The assets of this old and honorable organization in the United States alone reaches $1,848,609, and the net surplus of the American branch foots up $855,621. In addition to its United States assets, the unlimited resources of the society, together with the individual responsibility of its shareholders, is such as to entitle it to the utmost respect and confidence. Age, wealth, stability and upright dealing have given it an enviable reputation.

LA FONCIERE MARINE INSURANCE COMPANY,

OF PARIS, FRANCE,

Is one of the best known foreign marine companies in the world and dates its organization from 1879. Its policies are negotiable in all the moneyed centers of the world.

LONDON AND PROVINCIAL MARINE INSURANCE CO.,

OF LONDON, ENGLAND,

Was founded in 1860 with a subscribed capital of 1,000,000 pounds, and a paid up capital of 100,000 pounds. Under the guidance of its secretary, J. L. Daniel, it is one of the ablest managed of the English marine companies.

Hutchinson & Mann also represent the Hartford Steam Boiler Inspection and Insurance Company and the Metropolitan Plate Glass Insurance Company, both of which rank foremost in their respective lines.

Prussian National Insurance Company.

OF STETTEN.

SO well known is the standing of the Prussian National Insurance Company, not only in insurance circles but among property owners and business men throughout this section, that but little information can be added in regard to its financial standing and management. The last statement of the company shows that its capital is $2,250,000, and its assets $3,217,859, while its liabilities are but $451,361, leaving a surplus of $2,766,498. This statement is remarkable from the fact that no other insurance company doing business on this Coast can show so small an amount of liabilities as against an equal amount of assets. Merchants and property owners should study this matter carefully, for it is a well known fact that banks, insurance companies, or business houses should not be judged by the amount of their assets but by *the comparison between assets and liabilities.* The company was organized in 1845, and for nearly half a century has so conducted its business as to avoid all litigation and disputed claims. The company is the strongest German company represented on the Coast, and offers the utmost security to its policy holders. It commenced business in this section in 1881, and has rapidly forged its way to the front. The present general agents, Hirschfeld & Jacoby, have represented the company here since 1886, but Franz Jacoby was the general agent from 1884 when he succeeded his father who had for several years been its Pacific Coast representative. Mr. Jacoby has been engaged in the insurance business since 1879. He was for two years in the office of H. W. Syz, General Agent Swiss Marine Insurance Companies combined. In 1884, he as above stated, succeeded his father as General Agent of the Prussian National. David H. Hirschfeld, while not so long in the business, brings to the firm a reputation for energy gained in a long career as a merchant and manufacturer on this Coast. The company they represent is reliable and conservative and their many agents throughout this section are yearly adding to the list of policy holders.

The Union Fire and Marine Insurance Co.

OF NEW ZEALAND.

THIS corporation has a subscribed capital of $10,000,000, with a half million actually paid up; its net surplus over and above liabilities, including capital, amounts to $163,643.53. Since its incorporation the Union has paid losses amounting to nearly $3,000,000, and to its head office management, consisting of Hon. John T. Peacock, M. L. C., Chairman, George G. Shead, Vice Chairman, W. Devenish Meares, General Manager, can be credited the steady growth and success of the corporation. The company about six years ago opened a branch office in this city, investing its premiums over and above losses and expenses in San Francisco, thus localizing its business; in addition the Union has voluntarily invested in our securities until the fund now exceeds $150,000. The management of its United States branch is in the hands of L. L. Bromwell, 318 California street, assisted by a local Board of Trustees, comprised of Henry Wadsworth, Daniel Meyer, and John D. Vost. The Union's fire and marine business in this field aggregates $150,000 annual premiums, and is steadily growing.

The New Zealand Insurance Company.

OF AUCKLAND N. Z.

THE New Zealand Insurance Company was established in Auckland, New Zealand in May 1859, with paid up capital of $24,225. In 1862 its paid up capital had increased to $75,000; in July 1863, to $150,000; in July 1864, to $225,000. In January 1865, to $250,000, in 1871 to $375,000; in 1873, to $500,000, to-day the paid up capital stands at $1,000,000, with assets over $2,600,000 with unlimited liability of shareholders.

The California branch was established in San Francisco in March 1875. About the end of 1877, a branch was established in Portland to manage the business of Oregon and Washington Territory, which has been for the past nine years under the management of Wm. F. Brownton. Quite recently a branch has been established in Los Angeles for the better working of the southern part of the State, under the management of George Bradbeer. During the period under review the New Zealand Insurance Company has had its years of prosperity and adversity in California business, the loss ratio during thirteen years averaging 32% on fire business and 46% on marine: the proportion being about two-thirds fire, and one-third marine business.

Apparently the returns have been satisfactory to George P. Pierce, the General Mananger at head office, Auckland, for, carrying out the same methods which obtain at other branches where business has been profitable, the company has invested part of the earnings of the San Francisco branch in a piece of real estate at No. 310, 312 and 314 California Street, running through to Halleck Street, with a frontage of sixty feet by a depth of one-hundred and twenty-four feet, which is valued at three hundred thousand dollars. Upon this it is intended to erect a handsome structure. Fifty thousand dollars in United States bonds are deposited with the Secretary of State in Oregon, for the protection of policy holders in that State, together making United States

HUGH CRAIG.

The New Zealand Insurance Company,

OF AUCKLAND, N. Z.

assets of about three hundred and fifty thousand dollars, in addition to which cash balances are kept at each of the branches.

The office for United States business is at No. 312 California Street, under the jurisdiction of Hugh Craig, who is the manager for the entire Pacific Coast States and Territories.

Hugh Craig was born in Australia, and at an early age removed with his family to New Zealand where his education was obtained, and early in life he became engaged in the grocery trade and later in the lumber business. In 1870 he came to this State, and commenced life here as a laborer, working in the Oakland Planing Mills at $1.75 per day. He afterwards became Purser of the steamship Nebraska, Webb's Australian line. While in this position he received the appointment of manager of the Auckland Steam Packet Co., with headquarters at Auckland N. Z. In 1873 he resigned this post and returned to California and became accountant in the Oakland Planing Mills, where he had formerly worked as a laborer, remaining with the mills until 1875, when he was appointed Agent of the Pacific Coast Branch of the New Zealand Insurance Company. Proceeding to Auckland for instructions he later in the same year returned to San Francisco and opened his office, which under his judicious management has secured a large share of the underwriting business.

Insurance Company of North America.

"YE Insurance Company of North America" is the oldest company in America, having been organized in 1792. The home office is located in the city of Philadelphia, and general agencies have been established in all sections of the Union. The general agency of the Pacific Coast was established in 1872, and since that date it has taken a leading place in insurance circles. Its losses, which have been large, have been met with that promptness which has ever characterized the policy of this company. The company has a cash capital of $3,000,000.00, a net surplus over and above capital of $2,530,329.36, and cash assets of $8,474,351,88. Its 186th semi-annual official exhibit for January 1st of the past year showed as follows;

ONE HUNDRED AND EIGHTY-SIXTH SEMI-ANNUAL STATEMENT OF THE ASSETS OF THE COMPANY JANUARY 1, 1887.

First Mortgages on Real Estate	$1,976,644 97
Real Estate, Philadelphia, Baltimore, Indianapolis and Erie.	363,603 39
United States Loans, and Loans of the State of New Jersey	98,450 00
Boston, Hartford, Baltimore and other City Loans	803,840 00
Pennsylvania, Philadelphia and Erie, Lehigh Valley, and other Companies' Bonds and Stocks	3,985,199 00
Cash in Bank and Banker's hands	485,349 87
Loans with Collaterals	16,199 00
Notes Receivable and Unsettled Marine Premiums	325,319 38
Net Cash Fire Premiums in course of transmission	230,038 47
Accrued Interest, and all other Property	161,224 64
Total Assets	$8,474,351 88

LIABILITIES.

Capital Stock	$3,000,000 00
Reserve for Re-Insurance	2,570,854 60
Reserve for Unadjusted Losses and other Liabilities	373,167 92
Surplus over all Liabilities	2,530,329 36
	$8,474,351 88

The large surplus in addition to its paid up capital of $3,000,000 is an item meriting the attention of property owners and business men. The company's business is widely scattered over the entire country, the Pacific Coast branch having agencies at all the important points in this and adjoining States and Territories. Thomas A. Mitchell, who is General Agent for the Pacific Coast Department, has served a full apprenticeship at the business, having entered the employ of the Pacific Insurance Co. of San Francisco in 1870, and when that company ceased business Jonathan Hunt, who had been President of the Pacific, appointed him special agent of the Insurance Company of North America and other companies of which Mr. Hunt had become General Pacific Coast Agent. In 1878 he was made co-partner in the Agency with Mr. Hunt and so continued until 1886, when Mr. Hunt retired on a pension granted by the Insurance Company of North America and Mr. Mitchell became the general agent.

Manheim, Staples & Co's. Agency

SCOTTISH UNION AND NATIONAL INSURANCE CO.,

OF EDINBURGH.

By the report of the Insurance Commissioner for the year ended December 31st, 1886, the paid up cash capital of this company was $1,412,855.00, and its total assets were $16,975,146.40, divided as follows:

Real Estate	$ 930,345 46
Loans on Bonds and Mortgages	9,912,007 39
Stocks and Bonds owned by Company	3,641,793 08
Collateral Loans	1,541,687 44
Cash on hand	325,310 65
Interest due and accrued	108,386 19
Premiums in course of collection	477,485 73
All other Assets	28,130 46
Total	$16,975,146 40

This exhibit should be entirely satisfactory to those holding policies in this company. The company was organized in 1824, and commenced business here in July, 1881.

NATIONAL FIRE INSURANCE COMPANY.

OF HARTFORD, CONN.

The National Fire has a paid up capital of $1,000,000, and assets amounting to $1,958,506.83. The company commenced business in 1871, and was admitted into this State in 1884. In 1886 this company wrote in California risks amounting to $1,515,325.00, which is an evidence of its popularity throughout this section.

PROVIDENCE WASHINGTON INSURANCE CO.,

OF PROVIDENCE, R. I.

Was organized in the year 1799. It has a paid up capital of $400,000.00 and assets reaching $1,025,803.98. This company offers first-class security against loss by fire.

The steady progress of this popular company speaks well for it, and should commend it to the people of this State as a thoroughly reliable company.

Manheim, Staples & Co. are the general agents for the States and Territories west of the Rocky Mountains for the solid companies above named. The firm consists of Isaac Manheim, James W. Staples, J. Henry Dibbern and Henry S. Manheim, and are successors to Hagan, Manheim & Co., and have been for many years among the leading underwriters of this section. The firm have agents in all the prominent cities and towns in

COL. J. W. STAPLES.

this and surrounding States and Territories, and transact a large business. Their well-known integrity and promptness in adjusting losses, coupled with the high standing of the companies they represent, has made their agency a favorite with the insuring public.

Robert Dickson's Agency.

Mr. Dickson represents on the Pacific Coast three of the foremost English companies doing business in this country, in addition to which he also manages the Coast affairs of the Connecticut Fire Insurance Company of Hartford.

THE LONDON ASSURANCE CORPORATION.

Is the oldest company doing business in the United States, having been established by Royal Charter in 1720, and with the exception of the Hand in Hand and Sun, it is the oldest insurance company in existence. The corporation has a paid up capital of $2,241,000, and assets of about $17,000,000. It entered California in 1872, and has steadily advanced since that date.

THE NORTHERN ASSURANCE COMPANY,

OF LONDON,

Was established in 1836, and entered this State in 1862. The company has a paid up capital of $1,500,000, and assets reaching $17,000,000. The management of this company has been such as to commend it to property owners throughout this Coast, and secured for it a large patronage.

THE QUEEN INSURANCE COMPANY,

Dates its organization back from 1858, and commenced business in California in 1874. Its paid up capital amounts to nine hundred thousand dollars, while its assets foot up six and a half million dollars. An attempt to add to the reputation of the Queen, would be like "carrying coals to Newcastle."

The Connecticut Fire Insurance Company has its headquarters in the home of American insurance, Hartford, in which city it was organized some thirty-eight years ago. It offers as security for its risks a paid up capital of $1,000,000, and assets of $2,000,000, together with safe conservative management, prompt payment and liberal adjustments. For the past fifteen years it has been operating with success on this Coast, and like wine continues to improve with age.

Robert Dickson, the Pacific Coast Manager of these important companies, is a native of Scotland, and came to California in 1866, entering the office of Cross & Co. as a clerk. In 1872 he was made the manager of that firm's insurance business, and continued in that position until 1877 when he became associated with W. Lane Booker in the management of the Pacific Coast Branch of the Imperial, Northern, London and Queen Insurance Companies. In 1882 Mr. Booker, who had been for many years her Britannic Majesty's Consul at this port, was promoted to the post of Consul-General for the United States, and as this necessitated his removal to New York, he withdrew from the firm leaving Mr. Dickson sole manager of the business, which, under his judicious management, has steadily increased. As an underwriter and a business man he enjoys an enviable reputation.

Geo. Marcus & Co's. Agency.

MANNHEIM INSURANCE COMPANY,

(MARINE) OF MANNHEIM.

IT is but natural that a large marine insurance business should be transacted along the Pacific Coast, and especially in San Francisco, the largest port of entry on the Pacific Ocean, and one of the most important in the world. Many of the most prominent marine insurance companies in the world have established agencies on this Coast, and among the leading ones may be noted the Mannheim Insurance Company of Mannheim. The capital of the company now stands at $2,000,000, and its reserve fund at $515,000. The promptness and fairness with which all the business of this company is transacted, has made it hosts of patrons.

THE STRAITS INSURANCE COMPANY (Ld.)

(MARINE) OF SINGAPORE.

With a capital of $3,000,000, a reserve fund amounting to $200,000, and a surplus beyond capital and all other liabilities reaching $352,073.95, the Straits Insurance Company offers to its many friends an absolute security from marine losses. That the policy of the company has been satisfactory to its patrons is shown by the fact that cash dividends are yearly paid ranging from 15 to 25 per cent. to its policy holders, on net premiums contributed.

TRANSATLANTIC INSURANCE COMPANY,

OF HAMBURG.

This company presents the following showing: capital, $1,500,000; surplus, $276,166.67; assets January 1st, 1887, $1,251,296.47, and of this amount $501,856.48 is invested in the United States. This is certainly a satisfactory exhibit, and one of which the company may well feel proud.

THE STRAITS FIRE INSURANCE COMPANY, (Ld.)

OF SINGAPORE.

The capital of the Straits Fire Insurance Company amounts to $2,000,000, and is entirely independent of the $3,000,000 capital of the Straits Insurance Company (Marine). The company does a fire business in all its branches, and is favorably known throughout this slope.

The General Agents of the above named companies are C. H. George Marcus and Fr. Hohwiesner, who transact business under the firm name and style of Geo. Marcus & Co. The agencies controlled by these gentlemen cover all the States and Territories west of the Rocky Mountains. In addition to insurance they are engaged in the importing and commission business.

Parrott & Company's Agency.

THE house of Parrott & Co., is so well known not only in San Francisco but all over the shipping world, that it is unnecessary in this paper which is devoted solely to insurance, to speak of their large business as shipping and commission merchants. The insurance department of the firm which is devoted to the marine branch of underwriting includes the

ALLIANCE MARINE ASSURANCE COMPANY (Ld.), OF LONDON,

Which was organized in 1824, and has been doing business on this Coast since 1881. The capital of the company is $5,000,000, of which amount $1,250,000 is paid in. Its assets reach $2,059,141.48 while its liabilities are only $382,142.81. The Alliance is by general consent one of the strongest companies taking marine risks on this Coast, and by its prompt and liberal business methods has succeeded in gaining the respect of shippers throughout the Coast.

CANTON INSURANCE OFFICE (Limited). OF HONGKONG, CHINA.

The annual statement of this company for the year ending December 31st, 1886, shows its capital to be $2,500,000, of which amount $500,000 is paid in. Its assets are placed at $1,301,317.70 and its total liabilities at $182,635,07. The company is one of the most popular doing business on this Coast, and its promptness in settling losses makes it an excellent company to place risks with. The cash dividends paid to policy holders on net premiums contributed during 1886, were twenty-five per cent.

THE LONDON ASSURANCE CORPORATION, OF LONDON,

Has a subscribed capital of $4,482,750, of which $2,241,375 is paid up, and cash assets amounting to $16,460,880. This is a sterling reliable and conservative corporation, and one that has for many years occupied a leading place in insurance circles.

The insurance branch of Parrott & Co's., extensive business is in charge of Henry H. Nagle as Manager, and the firm are to be congratulated upon securing his services. While a native of New Zealand, Mr. Nagle arrived here early in 1851, when but a boy. Reared and educated in San Francisco, he became engaged in various enterprises until 1870, when he entered the service of the Union Insurance Company of this city, with whom he remained until 1881, when he was offered and accepted the management of Parrott & Co's., insurance business which he has since conducted to the entire satisfaction of the general agents and the home officers. He enjoys the reputation of being a painstaking reliable business man, an experienced and conservative underwriter and a courteous and pleasant gentleman.

Pacific Mutual Life Insurance Company.

OF CALIFORNIA,

WAS organized in 1867, and transacts both a life and accident insurance business.

Its principal office is located in the handsome building, No. 418 California street, in this city.

The officers are George A. Moore, President; George W. Beaver, Vice-President; W. R. Cluness, M. D., Medical Director; J. N. Patton, Secretary; Samuel M. Marks, Assistant Secretary; William O. Gould, Actuary; Thomas Bennet, General Superintendent; Charles N. Fox, attorney; and the following well-known citizens compose its Board of Directors: Robert Sherwood, George W. Beaver, L. S. Adams, Columbus Waterhouse, W. T. Garratt, W. R. Cluness, Samuel Leavensen, George A. Moore, J. F. Houghton, Hugh M. Larue, D. W. Earl, Charles N. Fox, L. P. Drexler, James Carolan and Henry T. Scott.

The Pacific Mutual is the only life and accident insurance company organized under the insurance laws of the State of California, and the only one transacting business in the United States whose stockholders are by law made liable for the debts of the corporation and whose directors are made responsible for the acts of officers.

This, together with the sound and progressive condition of the company and its just and prompt dealings, accounts for its popularity, growth in business and large assets. During the twenty years of its existence it has paid upon policy holders' account $3,600,000, it has loaned to citizens of this Coast some $4,700,000 and it now holds invested, according to law and for the security and protection of its policy-holders, $1,687,814.

The fact that the company has never called in a loan, where the security remained unimpaired, has made it very popular among borrowers, so much so that it finds no difficulty in obtaining choice mortgage loans at an advance upon the interest rates obtainable by other money-loaners.

Its policies, both life and accident, contain provisions against forfeiture, impose no restrictions upon residence or travel, and provide for immediate payment on presentation of satisfactory proofs of claim. Its life policies contain the indisputable clause and contain no conditions as to occupation or employment after the second year.

GEORGE A. MOORE.

The prompt manner in which it pays claims is *particularly noticeable*, its policies providing for *immediate payment* upon the furnishing of satisfactory proofs. Whenever such proofs are deposited with the company, and due form of receipt is ready, the company is ready to, and does, pay the claim. Of all the death claims paid by it in 1887 the average time between filing of complete proofs and payment was but *four* days.

The formation of the company is peculiar and exceedingly favorable to policy-holders, as the stockholders, though liable for all the debts of the corporation, are limited in their profits to the interest actually earned by the capital stock. Every dollar paid in by policy-holders is for their benefit alone, and, after providing for the necessary expense and the legal reserve fixed by law, all the remainder is returned to them, or their representatives, in the shape of policy-claims and dividends.

George A. Moore, the President of the corporation, is a native of Philadelphia, Penn., and is now in the fifty-fourth year of his age. During the past thirty years he has been continuously engaged in insurance, in the inland marine and fire, as well as the life and accident branches of the business. He is a thorough business man, and this with his knowledge of the details of his profession and the possession of executive ability, accounts for his own and his company's success.

J. N. Patton, the Secretary of the Company, was born in Ohio, is forty-three years of age and has been connected with the Pacific Mutual since 1877, and has served in his present capacity as Secretary since the spring of 1882.

For a number of years prior to coming to California, Mr. Patton was engaged in the business, serving for a number of years in important positions, first in the Missouri Valley Life Insurance Company's home office, and later in the office of the Alliance Mutual, of which last Company he was for several years Secretary. As a careful, accurate, methodical and thoroughly reliable office man, he has few equals and no superiors.

J. N. PATTON.

The Home Benefit Life Association.

HAS incorporated 1880 under the laws of the State of California, and is a mutual life insurance association, managed on business principles in the interest of its members. Its principal features are that it furnishes life insurance at as small an expense as security to the insurers and safety to the company will allow, and collects installments at definite dates written in the policy. Its policies are definite contracts for the full amount written therein, and free from all technicalities and burdensome conditions. The association

OFFICE THE HOME BENEFIT LIFE ASSOCIATION.

confines its business to life insurance, and is not engaged in banking. Its reserves are deposited in the San Francisco Savings Banks at interest compounding semi-annually. It insures *men* only. Its installment rate is based on the American Experience Table of Mortality, averaged for each period of five years; thirty-three and one-third ($33\frac{1}{3}$) per cent. for reserve and expenses of administrations added thereto. The total payments thereon, in excess of mortality and actual expense, are applied to the direct benefit of persistent members in reducing future cost. Its membership is composed of the leading business and professional men of the Coast, the majority of its members being in and near the city of San Francisco, where it is best known. It has paid promptly and in full nearly $400,000.00 in death claims, without expense to beneficiaries.

[Extract from the Report of the Examining Committee.]

SAN FRANCISCO, January 5, 1888.

To the Officers and Members of the Home Benefit Life Association:

GENTLEMEN:—After a most thorough, careful and exhaustive examination of the books of your Association for the year 1887, we take great pleasure in certifying to the correctness of the same.

We find all death claims against the Association have been paid on or before the date they were due. We find the Reserve Fund has all been deposited in the San Francisco Savings Union and earning the high rate of interest paid by that bank on Term Deposits.

We find the business of the Association has increased over forty per cent. during the year.

We most heartily commend the management of the Association and congratulate the policy holders that it rests in such able and painstaking hands.

SAM'L D. MAYER, *with Commercial Union Assurance Co., Ld.* W. R. TOWNSEND, *with Wm. T. Coleman & Co.* GEO. H. MURDOCK, *of Swain & Murdock, Insurance Agents.*	Examining Committee.

Trustees: W. H. Chickering, Olney, Chickering & Thomas; Sidney M. Smith, Pres. Cutting Packing Company; George T. Hawley, Hawley Bros. Hardware Co.; E. C. Sessions, Pres. Oakland Bank of Savings; Charles H. Fish, Pres. Con. Va. Mining Co.; William H. Quinn, Huntington, Hopkins & Co.; Ambrose Cornwall, Oakland; Chas. L. Watson, W. & J. Sloane & Co.; Hon. Wm. H. Jordan, Supreme Master, A. O. U. W.; Hon. T. C. Coogan, Att'y. State Harbor Commissioners. President, Frank C. Havens; Vice-President, J.S. Byington; Secretary, A. S. Barney; Auditor, I. P. Allen, late of Bank of California; Medical Director, C. N. Ellinwood, M. D.; General Agents, L. B. Hatch, J. W. Howell; Treasurer of Mortuary Fund, Bank of California; Treasurer of Reserve Fund, San Francisco Savings Union.

F. C. Havens, the President of the Association, was born at Sag Harbor, N. Y., in 1848. In 1864 he sailed for China, and after two years on the Canton River steamers, started for this coast and reached San Francisco in February, 1866. He soon found employment in the Clay Street Bank in a minor capacity and rapidly rose to the post of teller, which position he resigned in 1876 to engage in the brokerage business, as a member of the San Francisco Stock and Exchange Board. In 1880, in connection with A. S. Brownell, a well and favorably known underwriter and actuary of New York, he organized the Home Benefit Life Association and acted as its general agent until 1886, when he was elected its President, which position he has since retained with credit to himself and increasing satisfaction to the trustees.

F. C. HAVENS.

Bankers and Merchants Mutual Life Association

OF THE UNITED STATES.

THE inestimable superiority of the Natural Premium Plan of Mutual Insurance over all others has been too fully demonstrated to need any extended notice here. The Bankers and Merchants Mutual Life Association of the United States was organized in 1885, and has from its inception achieved a most gratifying success. To-day its members are found all over the United States, and its able management and prudent conservative policy have secured for it the respect and esteem of all.

The company levied but two assessments in 1886, and but one in 1887 to June 1st, and all claims against the association have been paid in full.

No insurance company in this or any other country has ever failed by reason of the death rate experienced. The failure in

Bankers and Merchants Mutual Life Association
OF THE UNITED STATES.

each instance has been caused by peculation or speculation on the part of the management. The safeguards introduced render both impossible in this association. Life insurance, under any and all systems, consists in collecting from the living to pay the representatives of the dead. The system inaugurated by this association does this simply, directly and inexpensively. This association is purely mutual. No stockholders absorb profits, and no trustees divide surplus. Its members have a voice and vote in the management. Their books and papers are open for inspection and examination, and members are invited to investigate for themselves. A local board of trustees, composed of not less than ten leading citizens of each county, may be formed, who shall act as advisory counsel in the settlement of claims by the death of members. The plan of this association favors insurance for protection, and when its mission is accomplished, *i. e.* when the family shall have grown up, the member can retire without loss. The certificate of membership is free from objectionable technicalities.

ALEXANDER BADLAM.

The home offices in the Safe Deposit Building on Montgomery street, are elegantly fitted out and arranged with every facility for promptly and systematically carrying on the business, and in the various departments eleven assistants are employed. The officers are gentlemen of high standing, and in every way identified with our city's best interests. They are: Alexander Badlam, President; Gen. W. H. Brown, Vice-President; H. S. Sanders, Secretary; Richard K. Allen, General Manager; H. R. Houghton, Actuary; Jos. D. Redding, Counsel; and Dr. Wm. P. Sprague, Medical Director. Directors: Alexander Badlam, Thos. R. Hayes, Gen. W. H. Brown, H. S. Sanders, and R. K. Allen. Conducted, as this enterprise is, on the broad plane of mercantile honor, its future growth is assured.

The Travelers Life and Accident Insurance Company.
OF HARTFORD, CONN.

THIS Company has been doing business for over twenty-four years, and is one of the most popular and enterprising company's in America. It is constantly paying claims in both departments, and has paid to its patrons over $13,000,000. It is the largest and strongest Accident Company in the world, and its policies are scattered far and wide. It has insured over 1,500,000 men, and its policies grant the largest and most *unparalleled benefits*. As the company grows in years, and its business increases, it is constantly enlarging its benefits and new features under its contracts. Its accident policies now cover one-third of the principal sum in the event of the loss of a hand or a foot, and all of the principal sum in case of loss of two feet or two hands or one hand and one foot, or the entire sight of both eyes. It has the most liberal non-forfeitable life policy in the market, and with the term, paid up, and cash values given in every policy, and the low non-participating rates, it suits every one. Every year shows a steady increase in both departments, and the company certainly has a very bright future. Its accident tickets cover the same liberal features of its yearly accident policies, and can be found at every railroad or general ticket office on the continent, and for the small outlay for first-class insurance, no one

The Travelers Life and Accident Insurance Company.

OF HARTFORD, CONN.

can afford to travel without them. This company never discounts a claim, but pays cash in full on all legitimate claims. The company is under the same management as when first organized. James G. Batterson, President, is one of the ablest financiers in America and has no equal, and with Rodney Dennis, Secretary, John E. Morris, Assistant Secretary, Geo. Ellis, Actuary, and Major E. V. Preston, Superintendent of Agencies, the affairs of this company are handled in a safe and very conservative manner, and the future prosperity of the company is assured. During the year just closed the company shows an increase in accident premiums over the previous year of $170,000, and the gain of its Pacific Coast department is creditable, which embraces seven States and Territories, and has over five hundred agents doing a good business in all departments. For the past three and one-half years the Pacific Coast General Agency has been handled very successfully by Walter W. Haskell, who with his extensive acquaintance over the entire Coast, enables him to place this company in every locality where business can be secured, and the constant increase in its business shows that attention to business brings its reward. Quick and active in all things Mr. Haskell never lets an opportunity pass to strike a blow for his company, and by his honorable business methods has gained the esteem, not only of the public but his competitors in the business. An excellent picture of this popular and painstaking agent is given in the next column. Thousands have had their experience, and say, "Always safe when insured in The Travelers."

WALTER W. HASKELL.

The Equitable Life Assurance Society.

OF THE UNITED STATES.

THE Equitable Life Assurance Society was organized in New York City in 1859, at a time when life assurance, although long practiced in England, was but little appreciated in this country. It is now acknowledged that its advent marked the commencement of a new era in the business of assuring lives. It rose rapidly to prosperity, and soon acquired an influence and a leadership which it maintains today. Its business management, from the start, has been cautious, practical and honorable, never requiring a retrograde step. Scarcely any changes have been made in its administration. Many of the directors and executive officers, connected with it when it occupied a small office at 92 Broadway, are connected with it now. It was soon crowded, by pressure of business, into larger, and then again into still larger premises, and it has been finally compelled to construct apartments, especially designed to accommodate its increased business, in that imposing granite edifice, which now ornaments Broadway, from Cedar Street to Pine Street, where it is destined to promote, by the extension of life insurance, that private happiness and national prosperity which is its natural result. The Equitable is today the strongest and most prosperous institution of its kind, because it has more outstanding assurance on its books, a larger annual business, and a larger surplus than any other company in the world.

The Equitable Life Assurance Society,

OF THE UNITED STATES.

The Pacific Coast branch has long ranked foremost in life insurance circles. The offices located on Montgomery street, give employment to a full force of trained assistants. North & Snow are the managers for the entire Pacific Coast. They are gentlemen who possess a thorough practical knowledge of the business in its minutest details, and to their efficient management is due the success which has attended this branch. The Equitable Life Insurance Company is too well known to require any extended notice here. Its conservative policy, honorable methods, and promptness in settling all losses have secured for it the respect of all. The Pacific Branch is one of the most important and successful, and will doubtless grow in a proportionate ratio with the city and State of which it is so important a component.

The ledger assets of the company on the 1st day of January, 1886, amounted to the enormous sum of $62,087,513.85, while its income from premiums, rents and interest for the year 1886, brought its assets on January 1st, 1887, to $81,961,247.04. The company paid out to policy holders during that year $8,336,607.90. The new insurance written during 1887 footed up $138,000,000. Its assets today stand at $83,000,000.

These figures render words unnecessary.

United Life and Accident Insurance Association.

PACIFIC Coast agency 312 Pine Street, San Francisco, Cal. Geo. R. Sanderson, General Agent; D. H. Allen, Manager; Wm. M. Lawlor, M. D., Medical Examiner. The United Life and Accident Insurance Association was incorporated under the laws of the State of New York in December, 1885, since which time it has written 2,659 policies, insuring the enormous amount of $12,113,000. It has paid death claims amounting to $37,000, and accidental indemnity to the amount of $6,119.65. All claims have been paid promptly and in full. This association combines in one policy life and accident insurance, charging no more for both, than the usual assessment companies charge for life insurance alone. It gives its members insurance at actual cost as no assessments are made for any purpose other than the payment of death losses. Any balance remaining over from an assessment after the payment of claims for which the assessment was levied, goes to the "Mortuary Fund" to meet the payment of the next loss. Expenses of every kind and all accident benefits are paid out of the annual dues. Only the annual dues are made payable in advance, other calls upon the pockets of its members being made only when needed, to pay the death claim of some fellow member. A rigid medical examination, and a careful scrutiny of all applicants insures a low rate of mortality, while an honest and efficient management by a Board of Directors consisting of men well known in New York business circles, is a guarantee to any one desiring insurance of the value of a policy issued by the association. The United Life and Accident has a large and rapidly increasing membership on this Coast, representing men prominent in all the walks of life.

GEO. R. SANDERSON.

The association began business January 2d, 1886. During that year it has issued 1,352 policies, and during 1887 it has written 1,307 policies, making a total of 2,659 policies, aggregating $12,113,000 of insurance.

There have been but five assessments during the two years from which there has been realized the sum of	[illegible]
Of this Mortuary Fund there has been disbursed in payment and adjustment of Death Claims	40,327 94
Leaving to the credit of the Fund a balance of	14,549 61
There has also been paid account of Accident Claims $6,855 leaving to the credit of the Accident Fund a balance of	1,360 50
Making to the credit of the two Funds a total of	16,210 11

www.ingramcontent.com/pod-product-compliance
Lightning Source LLC
Chambersburg PA
CBHW020335090426
42735CB00009B/1545
9783743344709